Kabbalah

THIS IS A CARLTON BOOK

Text and design copyright © Carlton
Books Ltd 2005

First published in 2005.
This paperback edition published in 2012
by Carlton Books Ltd
20 Mortimer Street
London W1T 3JW

10 9 8 7 6 5 4 3 2 1

A CIP catalogue for this book is available
from the British Library.

ISBN 978-1-78097-178-0

Editor: Penny Craig
Art Editor: Zoë Dissell
Design: Anita Ruddell
Picture Research: Sarah Edwards
Production: Janette Burgin

Printed in Dubai

Kabbalah

An introduction to the esoteric
heart of Jewish mysticism

Tim Dedopulos

CARLTON

Contents

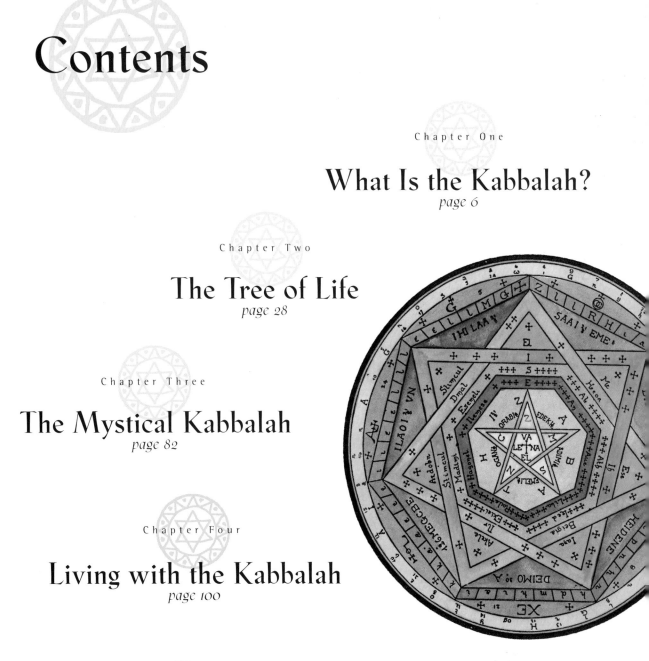

Chapter One

What Is the Kabbalah?
page 6

Chapter Two

The Tree of Life
page 28

Chapter Three

The Mystical Kabbalah
page 82

Chapter Four

Living with the Kabbalah
page 100

Resources
page 124

Index
page 126

Picture Credits
page 128

What Is the Kabbalah?

The ancient mystic wisdom of the Jewish faith is many things: a map that shows the path to self-perfection; an elegant model of the psyche; the heart of the western mystery tradition; a perfect system of correspondences; God's blueprint for creation; the key to unlocking your ultimate potential .... The Kabbalah is all these things and more – a vibrant body of mystical techniques and teachings that can help unlock the true meaning of life, the universe and, well, pretty much everything.

The Teaching of Tradition

The word "Kabbalah" is derived from a Hebraic root word that means "to receive," "to accept," and by common usage, "tradition." Looking at the various meanings of the word gives us our first clues. Tradition is that which is received and accepted – in other words, knowledge, passed down over the millennia. The knowledge itself is tradition; the teacher just a vessel. This, then, is the nature of the Kabbalah: the first and ultimate knowledge, greater than any master. It takes the form of a large body of teachings – written, oral and practical – about the nature of God himself, the birth of the soul, the process of the creation of the universe, the purpose of life on Earth, and what happens afterward. In addition to the wisdom it contains, the Kabbalah also gives specific techniques for improving your mind, body, soul and life.

RIGHT: **Limitless Light: in Kabbalistic thought, all the universe and the diversity of life within it springs from the light of God's love.**

Many different groups have adopted and worked with the Kabbalah over the centuries. Ever since the Italian Renaissance masters in the fifteenth century first sought to master the compelling power of the Kabbalah from a Christian viewpoint, a steady stream of European knowledge-seekers has influenced its development – alchemists, Gnostics, Freemasons, Rosicrucians, ritualists, Theosophists and more. Each of these groups has developed the tradition in unique ways.

In the meantime, the traditional Kabbalah has remained strong within Judaism, developed by careful researchers, heretical visionaries and everyone in between. All this different input into the tradition has given it real vibrancy and life. As in every school of thought, there are competing viewpoints, rivalries and jealousies, but the Kabbalah itself benefits from the debate, growing ever stronger. Its greatest gift to the world, perhaps, is its compelling vision of inclusive religious experience. The Kabbalah does not try to identify and label God, nor does it preach about beliefs. Instead, it assures the seeker that it is possible to experience God for oneself, and it offers techniques for going ahead and doing just that.

A Guide to the Kabbalah

This book will take you on a grand tour of all the Kabbalah's many rich aspects. This chapter, *What is the Kabbalah?* looks at the history and development of the tradition, from its early beginnings 3,000 years ago, through the golden Kabbalistic ages of the twelfth and fifteenth centuries, to more modern times. It will also look at the most important strands of divergent thought from the Judaic teachings, including the "Cabbala" of the Gnostic Christians and the "Qabala" of the Hermetic mages.

The second chapter, *The Tree of Life,* introduces the heart of the Kabbalah, and of the universe itself. The *Otz Chiim*, or Tree of Life, is the sacred centre of Kabbalistic teaching, the framework upon which everything else hangs. It is the pattern by which God created the universe – and by which the soul itself is born – as well as the structure by which all things can be understood. The Tree of Life consists of ten *Sephiroth*, or spheres of influence, linked by 22 paths, or *Nativoth*. Understanding the Tree of Life is the key to perfection of the self and mastery of the world.

In the third chapter, *The Mystical Kabbalah,* we will look in greater detail at the various schools of thought that have integrated the Kabbalah, and the use that they have made of its mysteries. We will also examine the psychology of magical and mystical mindsets, and look at the way the Kabbalah has influenced, guided and been linked to the tarot since its very earliest times. In many important ways, the tarot is a manifestation of the Tree of Life, and understanding the one can greatly influence understanding the other.

Finally, the fourth chapter, *Living with the Kabbalah*, will bring things right up to date. We'll look at the Kabbalah as a modern phenomenon in its incarnation as a mystical path for the stars, and examine some of the ways it has adapted to modern times. Then to finish off, you'll discover a wide range of exercises and techniques that will help you put your new-found wisdom to work in your own life. The pinnacle of Kabbalistic work is the cultivation of "stillness" – that is, to refine and purify the self into a state of perfection, where true understanding of God, the universe and your own immortal soul can finally be unlocked.

Prepare yourself, for you are about to learn the deepest, most powerful secrets of creation itself.

The Beginnings of Kabbalism

The heart of Kabbalistic thought is nothing less than the most profound expression of humanity's desire to understand the divine – how can a mere mortal, flawed and unworthy, possibly find a way truly to know God and discern his purposes? This question has driven the development of the Kabbalah, taking it from its very earliest origins through to its current prominence.

This question is hardly unique to the Kabbalists. We all feel the need to find some sort of personal answer to the deepest questions of life, even if the answer some people choose is just that everything is a random coincidence. Every culture throughout history has come up with some sort of explanation as to how the world was created. The answers range from the very simple to the very complex, from *Fiat Lux* to the veils of *Maya*, or the mathematical intricacies of the Big Bang. There seems no doubt among us, as a species, that somewhere along the line, something was responsible, whether it was the First Word, the Sundering, or (as a new theory suggests) the accidental collision of a pair of 11-dimensional membranes.

The problem lies in working out exactly what it was that happened, and what we can do to find a point of contact, a way to break back into the infinite realms. One of the greatest modern scholars of the Kabbalah, Gershom Scholem, conceived of the structure of religion as something that had evolved over several discrete stages. In the first, "primitive" stage, religion does not admit any significant differentiation between the universe and the divine. Stars, heavenly bodies, storms, oceans, deep forests, all of these are direct and immediate aspects of the gods. When lightning strikes, the Thunder God is angrily smashing his fist onto the earth. When there is a solar eclipse, the Sun God is dying. This animistic attitude paints humanity as the plaything and victim of the divine – in close touch with the gods, but helpless in the face of their cruelties and whims.

The second stage is the "creational." in which God is responsible for the formation of the universe and everything it contains, but he is not part of it. There are many wonders in nature, but they are evidence of God's power and creativity, rather than a manifestation of his body. When the seas rise up, it is because God's winds are blowing, rather than because the sea itself is angry. Scholem saw this as Israel's unique contribution to world theology. In this model, God is all-powerful and all-loving, but withdrawn from the world. Humanity can rely on God's mercy, but cannot get close to him, nor easily communicate with him.

The third and most advanced stage of religion is the "mystical", and it is the province of the Kabbalah. In this final form, the circle starts to close back toward primitive animism, but from the point of view of empowered understanding and loving communication. God's created are able to uncover the paths by which they can make their way back to God. They can therefore form very personal, open relationships with him; the Lord of All becomes the Loving Friend. By treading the paths of the orchard – that is, by studying the Kabbalah – the mystic

is able to finally come to the perfect relationship with divinity, in close contact with God, and certain of receiving his blessings.

The Kabbalah is a map and guide, but at the same time it is the territory itself. It represents the world, but also creates it and maintains it. The solid ground beneath our feet is formed by the interplay of the forces it describes, expressed and channelled through the Tree of Life. The Kabbalah is a description of creation, a blueprint for creation, and the very substance of creation itself, and all its complexities and intricacies have developed from that one fundamental question of how we can know God.

ABOVE: **Early man sought to tame the fury of nature by naming its elemental forces and worshipping them, hoping to win them over.**

RIGHT: **The Kabbalah manifesting through the Tree of Life was a powerful image for medieval esotericists, as this 1617 variant Tree of Life by Robert Fludd indicates.**

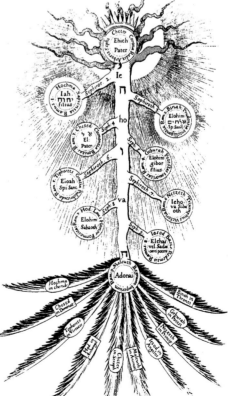

The Foundations of Kabbalism

The first recorded beginnings of the Kabbalah lie in the *Merkavah* school of Talmudic mysticism. Different Merkavah sages contributed important elements that would later become critical assumptions of the Kabbalah. An understanding of earlier Merkavah thought underpins the complexties of the Kabbalah. The Merkavah tradition was inspired by the prophet Ezekiel. The historical Ezekiel is thought to have lived around the sixth century BC. Still a child when the Babylonian kingdom of King Nebuchadnezzar forcibly deported thousands of important Israelites from their homeland, Ezekiel grew to become known as the prophet of the exiled peoples.

Despite his many miraculous feats, Ezekiel's main Kabbalistic importance lies in his vision of the "Merkavah," or chariot-throne, of God. In this extraordinary vision, Ezekiel describes a mighty disk of shining crystal that rolls on four multi-directional wheels of chrysolite. Each wheel is guided or accompanied by an angelic creature. A mighty throne of sapphire rests on the disk, and a figure in the form of man of bronze and flame sits upon it, surrounded by a brilliant rainbow glow. The many details of the vision have inspired debate over the millennia, but the most critical part of the vision was the implication that the divine presence on Earth was not restricted to the House of God at the Temple of Solomon. Instead, God could be seen and felt anywhere and everywhere, for those that had the eyes to see. Prior to Ezekiel's vision, it was assumed that God could only be known in his House – that only the priestly elite could ever approach him. Ezekiel turned this elitism on its head.

This revolutionary implication enlivened scholars and mystics for centuries to come, and kindled the thirsty speculation that gave rise to Merkavah mysticism – taking its name from the chariot of the vision. The mystics Ezekiel

ABOVE: **This seventeenth-century woodcut depicts the splendour of Ezekiel's vision of the Merkavah – the Chariot of God.**

LEFT: **A pair of Talmudic scholars debate a text in a *Yeshivah* – an academy for advanced study of the Talmud and other works.**

described a huge horde of them helping to do God's will: "a hundred thousand times a hundred thousand, ten million times ten million, an innumerable and uncountable multitude." Seven out of this vast host, in particular, he named as archangels – Michael, Raphael, Gabriel, Uriel, Raguel, Zerachiel and Remiel. The first four are usually identified with the angelic beings from Ezekiel's vision. According to legend, at the end of his life Enoch himself did not die, but was transformed into a pillar of living flame and reborn as the angel Metraton, high priest of the heavenly temple and minister of wisdom to the throne of glory.

Another important thread arose in the *Book of Jubilees*. This work was supposedly written down by Moses, who in turn was told what to write by an anonymous author, a mystic who had received its words from the Angel of the Presence. The book divides history into 50 periods of 50 years each, and reveals that God has a specific plan for history, no matter how complex it may seem. Hints of this purpose and destiny are revealed through complex patterns of numerology – a concept that still remains critically important to pure Kabbalistic thought.

Other key concepts were lost for millennia. The Dead Sea Scrolls, found in 1947 but dating back to the second century BC, described among other things the researches and teachings of the Essenes, who referred to themselves, within the sect, as the Sons of Light. They believed that the goal of spirituality was to purify themselves and the "fountain" of light within, and so reach a state of supreme perfection and godliness. At the same time, they were to strive against the impure, the Sons of Darkness, so as to try to bring light to the world and make it fit for God's rehabilitation. The greatest purpose of the

inspired literally sought to find out how God could be discovered. This, in turn, gave birth to the Kabbalah.

Over the centuries, the Merkavah sages reasoned that God could not corrupt himself by having contact with the impurities of the Earth. A whole host of beings was required to act as middle-men for him – angels, known at the time as "workers," or mal'akhim. They were first revealed to mankind through the prophet Enoch. The Book of Enoch

angelic host is to bring instruction – the mysteries of truth – to humanity. The Essenes saw evil as part of God's grand plan; not a rebellion, but a vital duty on the part of the evil angels.

The Wisdom of Akiva

Building on all these various layers of thought, one of the most important Merkavah sages was a second-century-AD rabbi named Akiva. An unassuming shepherd, Akiva did not even learn to read until the age of 40, when he was inspired to dedicate himself to study and meditation. Over the course of 15 years, he rose to become the leader of his people. Judea had been laid waste by the Romans, and when the rabbinical court, the *Sanhedrin*, moved to a town in Galilee, Akiva was placed at its head. With the position came the authority to pronounce on past laws and learning, and confirm or deny each new interpretation of the law.

Akiva believed that every letter, punctuation mark and even decorative flourish of the Holy Scriptures had been inspired by God, and that the study of such minutiae could reveal the truths of God's laws. Tales at the time claimed that three of the leading sages of the period came to Akiva for assistance in approaching God, and together, the four were able to do so. The four rabbis ascended into the orchard – that is, they undertook the secret teachings of the Kabbalah – and as they did so, Rabbi Akiva warned his fellows to discard any lingering notions of the pagan Greek theory that the universe was constructed from water. When they arrived at the pure marble stones of God's throne, the four rabbis gazed in awe. Rabbi Zoma's mind snapped, and he became instantly mad. Rabbi Azzai dropped as dead as a stone. Rabbi Abua became a murderous heretic in later life: it is historically documented that he was convicted of killing a young girl). Only Rabbi Akiva had the strength and purity to enter in peace and leave in peace.

Akiva's study of numerology and other forms of textual manipulation eventually led him to announce that he had found Israel's deliverer as prophesied in the Book of Numbers, a messianic military leader he renamed Simon bar Kochba – the "son of the star." Eventually, bar Kochba led the Judeans in a fierce revolt against Rome, and although the rebels inflicted terrible losses on the Roman legions, they were crushed. Rabbi Akiva was captured and tortured. His response was to ignore the pain and stoically chant his final Sh'ma. God delivered him from his trials, and he passed over.

With Akiva's death – and the loss of almost all of the Judean scholars – the Merkavah tradition lost a vital part of itself. Despite its faltering, however, it retained enough strength to give birth to the earliest piece of the Kabbalah proper, the *Sepher Yetzirah*, or Book of Creation.

Classical Kabbalism

It is almost certain that the *Sepher Yetzirah* was written during, or shortly after, the third century AD. Legend attributes authorship of the work to the biblical figure Abraham, the Chaldean patriarch from Genesis who was commanded by God to leave his native land for a destination that he would reveal along the way. As a historical figure, Abraham would have lived around 2,000 BC, but the *Sepher Yetzirah* is written in a clear, polished style of Hebrew consistent with the language of the third century AD. The work is referred to in several other ancient rabbinic tomes, which also restricts its minimum age; it is highly unlikely that so many other documents could be forged to retro-fit the book.

While the date of creation for the *Sepher Yetzirah* is comparatively certain, the matter of its authorship is entirely different. It was fairly common practice for sages at the time to lend weight to their opinions by attributing them to older, wiser figures. The habit continues to the modern day, of course – most recently, the popular '70s works attributed to the venerable Tibetan master Lopsang Rampa (*The Third Eye* was his biggest success) were eventually found to have been written by an unusually spiritual plumber from east London. Like the fictional Lopsang Rampa, wisdom could conveniently be attached to Abraham. The true author of the *Sepher Yetzirah* is now too distant in time and space ever to be discovered. It is a pity that the need for credibility has robbed the true author of his historical position as the founder of one of the greatest bodies of mystic thought in the world.

The *Sepher Yetzirah* is the foundation stone of the Kabbalah. It is written obscurely, full of poetic allusions and mysteries. It talks about the "thirty-two wondrous paths of wisdom engraved by God" in creating the universe: "thirty-two books, with number, and text, and message…Ten *Sephiroth* (spheres) of nothing, and twenty-two letters of foundation; three mothers, seven doubles, and twelve singles."

The rest of the book is dedicated to hints and teachings to help the student start understanding the nature of the ten Sephiroth and the 22 paths of knowledge that connect them. They form a scheme designed to help the human mind to understand how God relates to the real

BELOW: **The ten Sephiroth of nothing, as enumerated and depicted in the *Sepher Yetzirah* – their most ancient incarnation.**

LEFT: **After suffering many hideous trials at the hands of the Romans, Rabbi Akiva was buried in this historic tomb in Safed.**

ABOVE: **These modern Hasidic Jews are praying and making devotion at the Wailing Wall in Jerusalem – for Jews the most sacred place on Earth.**

world. Each individual Sephira is one element of God manifesting into the universe; as such, it is not finite, but contains an infinity within itself. Between them, the text states that they measure: "The depth of the beginning and the depth of the end, the depth of good and the depth of evil, the depth of the heights and the depth of the depths, the depth of east and the depth of west, and the depth of north and the depth of south – and one master, God, faithful King, rules them all from his holy place."

The spheres are not separate and self-contained however, but interlinked, later ones deriving from the earlier as God's mystery takes on form and meaning. According to the *Yetzirah*, they embody the four worlds of being. Understanding the Sephiroth and the Nativoth (paths) that link them is the great goal of all Kabbalistic work, but this must be approached in the proper manner, with an attitude of stillness in mind. We will discuss the Sephiroth and the Nativoth in the next chapter; for now, it is enough to remember that they are the most profound mysteries of all Kabbalism.

Hasidic Kabbalism

The next wave of Kabbalistic development did not begin until the twelfth and thirteenth centuries. Many Jews had been driven into Europe by Roman oppression over the centuries, and the joint hardships and opportunities of early medieval life in Central Europe bred a new skein of mysticism. Unlike traditional Jewish philosophy, which owed much to Aristotle and his school of thought, the *Hasidei Ashkenaz* (The Pious Ones of Germany) harkened back to the old Merkavah teachings. Where great mainstream Jewish philosophers such as Moses Maimonides were thinking about ways to deal with life and living, the Hasidim were teaching that God could be known, and that it was possible to make life into what you wanted, to be truly happy and contented.

The early leaders of the Hasidim were Rabbi Samuel he-Hasid (Samuel the Pious), Rabbi Judah he-Hasid, Samuel's son, and Eleazar ben Judah of Worms. They and their followers believed that the Word of God, as delineated in the Torah (the book of Mosaic law), could give the power to heal the flesh and drive out evil and sickness. Their teachings were recorded in the *Sepher Hasidim*, the "Book of the Pious." According to the book, the Word was hidden from plain sight, where only the worthy and pure could locate it, and the Hasidim devoted themselves to scrutinizing the Torah for hidden codes. Each mark and letter of the Torah was counted, analyzed, given a value and manipulated. Words that added to the same number were seen as equivalent at the least, and perhaps as revealing a special new wisdom. This technique was called *Gematria*, and its adepts were known as *Baal Shem*, "Masters of the Word."

The Baal Shem were noted for being practical Kabbalists, able to achieve mighty wonders through their understanding of the nature of creation. They taught others to make the most of life despite hardship, to be ascetic in physical needs and live as fully as possible in the higher spheres, without fear of death – for what was death but a return to God's side? It was a dark time for the Jewish people. Rampaging crusaders and Christian zealots resented the Jews' refusal to convert to Christianity. They stirred up mobs against Jewish communities, blaming them for the spread of plague and accusing them of poisoning drinking wells and kidnapping and murdering Christian children. In this poisonous atmosphere, the teachings of the Baal Shem offered hope and solace, and the movement flourished.

The Book of Brightness

The second great Kabbalistic treatise emerged from this darkness. The *Sepher ha-Bahir,* the "Book of Brightness," is as obscure in its exact attribution as the *Sepher Yetzirah*. The *Bahir* first appeared in the rabbinic academies of Provence in France. It was written mostly in Hebrew, with hints and elements of Aramaic, in a style that resembled the ancient *Midrash* commentaries. It was organized into sections, each with an introductory quote from a historic Merkavah sage – but so poorly structured that some scholars have suggested that the sheets of the book may have been accidentally shuffled before it was bound. The *Bahir* drew on Merkavah sources, the *Sepher Yetzirah*, the *Sepher Hasidim* and another ancient Talmudic text called the *Raza' Rabbah*, or "Great Secret", but it did much more than just collect earlier Kabbalistic knowledge.

The *Bahir*'s greatest contribution to Kabbalism was the image of a schema by which the Sephiroth could be interconnected, the Nativoth winding between them to form a perfect whole. The result was a diagram that illustrated God's model for creating the universe, and provided a clear road-map for humanity's re-ascension: the *Otz Chiim*, or Tree of Life. The Sephiroth clearly descended from the crown of perfect divinity (the Sephira *Kether*) to the earthly kingdom, *Malkuth*. But the *Bahir* also strongly introduced the concept of balance – for there to be harmony between the physical and the spiritual, there had to be harmony between the other polarities: male and female, severity and mercy, wisdom and understanding, good and evil. Just as the Tree of Life consisted of the

BELOW: **This esoteric variant of the Tree of Life clearly shows the balance of male and female and the formation of the archetypal human, Adam Kadmon.**

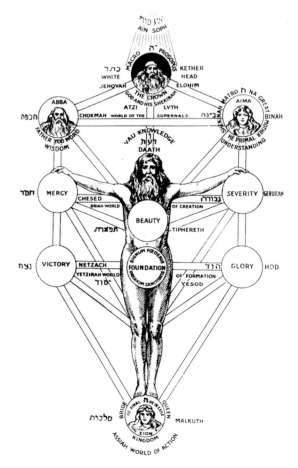

spheres of God's limitless bounty, so there was a reverse tree, a shadow side, made up of hollow husks, the *Qliphoth*, connected by dark paths indeed. Even this evil tree served God's purpose. Like the Merkavah mystics, the Bahir saw the forces of evil as a vital part of God's creation, working in his service.

The Spanish Renaissance

At the same time that the Hasidim were at work in Germany, the oral tradition of the Kabbalah was undergoing a renaissance in Spain. Its spearhead was a blind scholar named Rabbi Isaac ben Abraham, the son of a leading teacher of Jewish law. Isaac the Blind was a strong proponent of mystic secrecy, and taught almost exclusively by word of mouth. Even so, his Kabbalistic understanding was so profound that he is still known as the Father of Kabbalah. Isaac the Blind wrote one major text called *The Mystical Torah: Kabbalistic Creation*, which formed a commentary on the *Sepher Yetzirah*. It advanced understanding of the Creation and the divine nature of the universe by a significant margin, and gave clear exposition to the crucial Kabbalistic concept of *D'vikut,* "Cleaving" to God.

Isaac's teachings had powerful influence in shaping a circle of mystic thinkers and students in Gerona, near Barcelona. Two of the Gerona circle in particular, Rabbi Ezra and Rabbi Azriel, became prominent Kabbalistic writers, and their numerous works laid the foundation of inspiration for much of the mystic development that followed in the next two or three hundred years. Isaac the Blind was horrified, and wrote a stern letter to Ezra and Azriel, reproaching them for circulating Kabbalistic wisdom to the general public. They were persuaded to curtail their output, but the Kabbalah was no longer an obscure mystic discipline, but a significant part of Medieval Jewish life.

Other thinkers emerged, such as the Kohen brothers of Castille, who focused strongly on the nature of evil within the Kabbalah, and Abraham ben Samuel Abulafia, a nomadic mystic who wandered across Europe and even to the Holy Land in search of truths and answers. Abulafia's teachings had already made him famous, and

his journeys simply added further to his personal legend. He even visited Pope Nicholas III in Rome to demand an apology for the suffering that the Christians had inflicted on the Jews. The pope of course threw Abulafia straight into prison, but died before he could implement the death penalty that he had decreed. Eventually, Abulafia settled on a small, isolated island near Malta to continue working away from the world. His most notable contribution was an alternative decoding system to gematria (see above) called *tziruf*, which involved manipulating combinations of letters. He also left a system of meditation by which mankind could achieve D'vikut ("cleaving" to God) which still attracts attention today.

Another Kabbalistic wanderer was born at approximately the same time as Abulafia. Little is known of Moses de León's early life. At some point however, he came to possess a copy of Moses Maimonides' masterwork of Jewish philosophy, the *Guide for the Perplexed*. A brilliant, down-to-earth work about daily living, the *Guide* did not sit well with Moses de León, and he began his wanderings in Spain. During this time he came to know and learn from many of the Kabbalists and Gnostics active during the period. He wrote extensively on mystical matters, but found little success and next to no money.

Moses de León's fortunes changed when he announced that he had acquired a historical manuscript left behind by one of the leading sages from Rabbi Akiva's time, over a thousand years before. The supposed author of the manuscript, Simeon ben Yokhai, was a renowned Merkavic scholar, famed for secretly spending a dozen years hiding from the Romans in a cave with just his son for company. De León claimed that the manuscript had been found by a famous contemporary rabbinic scholar, Nachmanides. He had unearthed it in Palestine in the year 1265 and sent it to his son back in Catalonia. A magical whirlwind then descended from the heavens and snatched up the manuscript, bearing it across the land to Aragon, where Moses de León was waiting. As the new possessor of such ancient secrets, it was his solemn duty to distribute copies of the holy manuscript in time for the coming age of the Messiah.

The *Sepher ha-Zohar*, or "Book of Splendour," is an undoubted masterpiece of Kabbalistic thought. It is a vast

work, made up of several thick volumes crammed with commentaries and lectures. Medieval interest in the Kabbalah was peaking, and the *Zohar* arrived at exactly the right time, with exactly the right provenance. It was a stunning success, finally earning de León the literary and financial success he had craved for so long. It is still considered synonymous with the study of the Kabbalah. It collected all sorts of information from the oral tradition, elucidated confusing or conflicting points in the *Bahir* and the *Sepher Yetzirah*, and finally gave the Kabbalah the written record it needed to gain acceptance across Europe. While it did not actually add any new strands to Kabbalism, it did gather it all together, for the first time offering a significant and viable textbook to would-be mystics. It has held its prominence well, and studying the *Zohar* is still considered a prerequisite to achieving any serious mastery of the Kabbalistic tradition as a whole.

Eventually, one of Nachmanides' own pupils – who

ABOVE: **The *Zohar* is conveyed to Moses de Leon by divine providence in this illustration from the front of Von Rosenroth's commentary, *Kabbala Denudata*.**

had escaped the massacre of the Jews of Acre in Palestine – heard of the *Zohar* and came to Moses de León. It was the first that the survivor, Rabbi Isaac of Acre, had heard of an uncovered manuscript. Moses de León confidently repeated the story and invited Isaac back to his home in Avila to see the original manuscript. On the way back home however, de León fell ill. He was already 65 years old, and did not have the strength to fight off the disease; he died before being able to show the original *Zohar* text to Isaac.

In the furore that followed, Moses de León's wife and daughter stepped forward. They announced that Moses had been a genius in his own right, and that the *Zohar* had been entirely his own work, "forged" to help guarantee success. They maintained that there never had been a manuscript – and certainly, a modern linguistic analysis carried out by Gershom Scholem agrees that it is very likely that León wrote the whole thing. At the time though, the debate was fierce. Many of the book's adherents refused to accept the statement of de León's family, denouncing their testimony as self-interest and pride, and there are still thinkers who debate the book's provenance.

The Written Foundation

The written tradition of the Kabbalah crystallized around the *Zohar*. Along with the *Bahir* and the *Sepher Yetzirah,* it remains the foundation of Kabbalistic study. Isaac Luria, known as the "Divine Rabbi" and the "Lion," was a sixteenth-century sage who matured several of its ideas. Luria's doctrine of *Sheviret Ha Kelim,* or "The Shattering of the Vessels," stated that the moment of creation was the point where God, previously a single perfect unity, shattered himself into a multitude of holy sparks. These sparks shot out in a vast wave, becoming embodied in objects, beings and even actions. The similarity of Sheviret to the Big Bang is so striking that it

BELOW **French mystic and Kabbalist Guillaume Postel, 1510–1581, published Latin translations of the *Zohar* and *Sepher Yetzirah* before they were printed in Hebrew.**

ABOVE: **Even today, Safed remains steeped in history and antiquarian mystery, as befits the birthplace of the Kabbalah.**

hardly needs to be pointed out.

The notion of shattering led Luria to the doctrine of *Tikkun Olam*, Repair of the World. The shards of Holy Spirit yearn to return to unity with the source, to become part of God again. All things and actions are saturated with these holy sparks, awaiting the path of elevation that will lead to their release. The diaspora of the Jewish people served God's will, because the pure Jewish souls needed

to venture into other lands in order to help the holy sparks everywhere return to God's embrace. The goal of the Kabbalah, Luria claimed, was to facilitate the Tikkun. Luria's thinking had a strong influence on later Kabbalistic thought, finding particular favour in Gnostic theories.

There have been many commentaries and analyses since then, but little primary development of the Kabbalah. Christians and occultists have worked with the Kabbalah in deep and profound ways, but the pure source is still the material that sprang out of the golden age of Hasidic Kabbalism.

The Oral Tradition

But not all the Kabbalah is written. The oral tradition remained strong, and from time to time it has surfaced in the most spectacular ways. Israel ben Eliezer was born at the turn of the eighteenth century. A Hasidic *Baal Shem* (master of the word) miracle worker, he restored health, expelled demons, and taught – and brought – joy to his followers. His popularity was such that he was also named a Shem Tov, "one who has a good name". From the depths of poverty in southern Poland, he rose to inspire Jews all around the world, and became known

LEFT: **The Baal Shem Tov is shown here studying and teaching in a masterful painting by Shoshannah Brombacher.**

RIGHT: **One of the greatest Christian scholars and mystics, Saint Jerome, 347–419, was no stranger to asceticism, spending years at a time in the Syrian desert.**

as the first and only *Baal Shem Tov*, "master of a good Word." His followers elided this name, and eventually he became known as, simply, the *Besht*.

As a child, the Besht was a reluctant student. He was far more interested in wandering the woods, meditating on, and within, nature, where he felt most in touch with God. He was fascinated by the idea of learning to speak the language of nature, for he felt that nature was a pure link to God. Unsurprisingly, when he found the Kabbalah, he fell in love with it. He lived in simple purity and poverty,

giving away most of his income, and wandered the land, healing those in need. He is particularly famed for curing apparently incurable insanity, and he frequently employed Kabbalistic spells and amulets. At every opportunity, he taught others to become whole and balanced, embrace purity and happiness, and live in joy despite the sorrows of the world. It is said that he often literally danced with spontaneous joy.

After his death in 1760, Hasidic bands roamed across Europe, spreading their own versions of the Besht's

Gnostic Cabbalism

There are many elements of Kabbalistic thought that appeal to Christian mystics. The asceticism of the Hasidim struck chords with religious thinkers accustomed to self-denial, celibacy and mortification of the flesh. Their joyous worship is similar to that of Pentecostal Christianity. Furthermore, the notion of a hidden God approachable only through the understanding of sacred mysteries dovetailed well with the Gospel depictions of God as unknowable except through the life of Jesus. The idea of codes and ciphers hidden by God within a linguistic game, known as gematria, is highly transferable across any religious divide.

Gnostic mysticism had long been an influence on the development of the Kabbalah. Dating back to Greek schools of thought, Gnosticism can be defined as the search for knowledge that cannot be acquired through ordinary intellectual studies. It is the study, and acquisition, of secret and hidden doctrines that talk about the greater spiritual nature of the world. In Gnostic thought, the student must seek secret knowledge and mystical power as a way of achieving greater closeness with the divine. As such, Kabbalism had been a loosely Gnostic pursuit since its inception.

message. More orthodox Jews condemned the Hasidim, and there was significant tension for some time, but gradually the controversy died down. The Lubavitcher Hasidim, a Russian strain of Hasidic thought, sought to tone down the overt elements that had irritated other Jewish thinkers. This meant, in particular, being far more restrained about physical elements of the faith such as dancing, clapping and bobbing up and down. The Lubavitcher Hasidim came to dominate Hasidic thought, and make up the great majority of Hasidic Jews in the world today. In fact, the stereotypical image of a Hasidic Jew, with wide hats, black coats and visible prayer shawls, is specifically the Lubavitcher garb. The oral Kabbalah – and the miracle tradition of its practical application – is still alive and well, despite everything endured by the Jewish world over the last three centuries.

RIGHT: **Ramon Lull, 1232 –1316, was born in Majorca. A leading Franciscan and mystic scholar, his vision led to the earliest Kabbalistic/Christian fusions.**

LEFT: Count Giovanni Pico della Mirandola, 1463–1494. Pico vitalized the Italian Renaissance and popularized the Kabbalah. His early death was a great loss.

that, unlike many others, genuinely had been lost for centuries, the *Corpus Hermeticum*.

The *Corpus* was written in the first and second centuries AD, and was concerned with the mythic figure Hermes Trismegistus – another identity of Thoth, the Egyptian god of wisdom. It had long been believed that the *Corpus* described the true Egyptian religion, and that Thoth/Hermes was analogous with Moses. The date of the *Corpus*, and its strongly Neoplatonic nature, convinced scholars across Europe that Greek philosophy had in fact been a survival of ancient Egyptian religious and magical thinking. With Columbus's voyage of discovery underway, it was a time of great revelation for the Christian world. The Kabbalah burst out into this moment, carried by the exiled Spanish Jews, and Christian Gnostics leapt on it as the lost secrets that would allow access to the very innermost mysteries of the Bible.

Under the explicit guidance of the Medici family – who funded the Platonic Academy – the head of the Academy, Marcello Ficino, devoted the Academy's resources to translating and working with the *Corpus*. Pico della Mirandola was one of Ficino's students, and proved critical in bringing the Kabbalah into Gnostic Christian thought. He was convinced that Kabbalistic study – particularly gematria and the other analytical techniques – could verify the scientific truth of Christianity. He claimed to be able to prove, through manipulation of names and letters, that the Jewish Messiah was named Jesus: "No Hebraic Cabbalist can deny that the name 'IESU', interpreted on Cabbalistic principle, signifies the 'Son of God'".

Pico went on further, dividing the Kabbalah into two artificially distinct disciplines. One branch was concerned with passing messages to the forces of divinity, and the other was about harnessing the power of the angelic hosts. His efforts to publicize the Kabbalah as part of his quest to "prove" his ideas about Jesus were highly successful, and it is largely through his efforts that the mystics, scholars and thinkers of the time became familiar

The current flowed both ways, however. The first Christian scholar to incorporate the Kabbalah (or "Cabbalah," as Christian mystics have generally spelt it) into Christian thought was a thirteenth-century Spanish mystic, Ramon Lull. He devised an extraordinary system of wheels inside wheels that, he claimed, could allow the user to know everything that was going on in the universe. The rims of the wheels were inscribed with letters that stood for the ten qualities of God, which Lull claimed to have seen in a vision. These qualities were associated with, among other things, the ten Sephiroth, and ten of the most important Christian mythic figures. By manipulating the wheels, endless combinations could be formed.

Lull's work was built upon by an Italian scholar, a Florentine named Giovanni Pico, the count of Mirandola. Pico had become fascinated by the Kabbalah during the 1480s, enough to declare that "No science can better convince us of the divinity of Jesus Christ than the study of Magic and the Kabbalah." It was shortly after this – in 1492, the same year Columbus set sail for the New World – that the king of Spain banished all the Jews from his kingdom on pain of death. At the same time, the Platonic Academy in Florence obtained a bundle of manuscripts

RIGHT **English mystic Robert Fludd, 1575–1637, left a rich legacy of Kabbalistic and alchemical works. Here he is surrounded by some of his most important symbols.**

BELOW **A quasi-Kabbalistic "Tree of the Soul" showing the four worlds of creation, designed by German mystic and Kabbalist Jacob Boehme 1575–1624.**

with the concepts of Kabbalism.

The Jewish Kabbalists remained highly sceptical of Christian efforts to co-opt their tradition. There was significant fear that the interest would turn out to be another way of attempting to force conversion to Christianity. Their fears were somewhat allayed when Pico's life works inspired one of the brightest young stars of the German Renaissance, Johannes Reuchlin. Entranced with the Kabbalah, Reuchlin began seriously studying Jewish mysticism. He produced books on the Hebrew language and the Kabbalah, and was in the process of producing a work entitled *De Arte Cabalistica*, "The Kabbalistic Arts," when a converted former Jew, Johann Pfefferkorn, touched off a wave of hysterical anti-semitism in Germany.

Reuchlin – unimpeachably Christian – refused to back down, and entered into vitriolic debates with Pfefferkorn. The controversy became famous across Europe. Pfefferkorn was seen as a representative of the old guard, resisting the forces of the new progress, and Reuchlin became a hero. He went on to teach widely that the Christian Cabbalah was at the very core of the Renaissance, and that Hebraic study was as important as Greek. All over Europe, Christians turned respectfully to Jews to help gain true appreciation of the Old Testament and the Kabbalah.

It couldn't last. A wave of bigotry and hatred consumed Europe in the sixteenth and seventeenth centuries, culminating in the Great Inquisition and the witch trials. Anything that resonated of learning or the supernatural – or Jewish thought – was regarded as highly suspicious. Many scholars, mystics and healers

were tortured to death. The works of Cornelius Agrippa were the last gasp of Gnostic Cabbalism. His *Three Books of Occult Philosophy* were an attempt to combine Pico's Kabbalistic magic techniques with other, more natural magic. Agrippa felt the purpose of the Kabbalah was to fortify the soul for encounters with spiritual forces. Hatred and loathing of Agrippa – the most notorious "black magician" of the time – fanned the flames of Inquisition and witch-hunting across Europe. It was a

ABOVE: **Heinrich Cornelius Agrippa of Nettsheim, 1486–1535, was known as a knight, doctor and, by common reputation, a magician.**

cruel irony. Gnostic Cabbalism vanished underground with European mystics like Jacob Boehme and Robert Fludd, diffusing into general Renaissance thinking, hidden occultism, and alchemy. It remains in Christian thought today mainly as the study of angels and the angelic hosts.

Hermetic Qabalism

Alphonse-Louis Constant was born in Paris in 1810. He chose a career in the priesthood, but abandoned the seminary in 1836, having fallen in love with a girl he would later marry for a time. In 1841, Constant served an eight-month prison sentence for publishing a socialist work titled *The Bible of Liberty*. His interest in spiritual matters had always been strong, and he became fascinated by the occult. In 1845, he changed his name to a more Hebraic version of his forenames, Eliphas Levi, and dedicated himself to the study of magic and the Kabbalah. He became renowned as an occultist and necromancer, and even claimed to have summoned the spirit of Apollonius of Tyana (a Pythagorean philosopher and purported miracle worker supposed to have been a contemporary of Christ's) whilst on a visit to London in 1854.

Levi's greatest work, *Dogme et Rituel de la Haute Magie* ("The Dogma and Ritual of High Magic") was published in 1856. Other major works include *Transcendental Magic*, which is steeped throughout in esoteric Kabbalism, and *A History of Magic*. In *Dogma and Ritual*, Levi took a detailed look at the links between the Kabbalah and the tarot. As will be shown later, there is a strong possibility that the development of the tarot was strongly influenced by Kabbalistic principles and philosophies. Levi was not the first philosopher to discuss such links, but his work was certainly the most influential.

He was significantly interested in the Kabbalah in its own right. Levi considered it a more profound and powerful philosophy than all the others put together, a system that married the strength to bend the unseen world to the magician's will with a precision as exact as pure mathematics. He often claimed that there was a secret body of true magic at work right across the world, one that had shaped history through the actions of its adepts, and he apparently considered the Kabbalah to be the most likely suspect.

Eliphas Levi's work is the main reason you are able to read this book today. He alone inspired the massive occult revival of the late nineteenth and early twentieth centuries. Free at last from the murderous censure of

ABOVE: **Eliphas Levi, 1810–1875, was undoubtedly the father of the modern occult revival. Without his influence, this book would not exist.**

earlier times, and buoyed up by semi-legitimization from fledgling academic and medical fields like psychology and mesmerism, his fame, exploits and teachings were incendiary. Interest in the *ars occulta* exploded into a full occult revival – and the greatest product of the occult revival was a magical society called the Hermetic Order of the Golden Dawn.

The Golden Dawn taught a hodgepodge of magic and mysticism syncretized from hidden teachings and mystic exercises gathered from all around the world. They were united into a ceremonial magical tradition that has dominated western occultism ever since. Many important artists, writers and poets of the time were members of the Golden Dawn, and the society's teachings can be found in imagery right across the arts of the period. Levi, sadly, did not live long enough to see the Golden Dawn

LEFT: **Prankster, junkie, mountaineer, genius and self-proclaimed "wickedest man alive," Aleister Crowley hams it up for the camera.**

with degrees of initiation, all according to the perceived symbolism underlying the Kabbalah. There was a strong perception inside the society that all gods sprang from the same source. While all were one, part of the limitless light, different expressions of God could appear to be different deities. From there, it was obvious that across the world, certain deities – and qualities, and colours, and planets, and so on – were equivalent.

The Kabbalah was the key that unlocked this potential confusion. Building on Levi's work relating the ten Sephiroth and the 22 Nativoth to the tarot, the Hermetic researchers linked the Tree of Life to deities from ancient Greece and Egypt, to gemstones, to plants and flowers, and far more. This provided a foundation on which they could build their rituals and magical practices, and gave the Society an internal coherence that it would otherwise have lacked.

Undoubtedly, the original architects of the Kabbalah would have been deeply dismayed by the use that the Golden Dawn made of their work. However, it is possible to make a strong case that as the structure underlying God's creation of the universe, the Kabbalah *should* manifest itself within all cultures and belief systems. With that in mind, modern occultists have continued to build on the work of the Golden Dawn initiates, seeking to sharpen and extend the basis of correspondence.

The Golden Dawn's practices were supposedly secret, but after the society dissolved, Aleister Crowley exposed

he inspired; he died in 1875. That same year, however, saw the birth of the man who would go on to be the Golden Dawn's most notorious alumnus, variously described as a genius, a madman, a philosopher, an expert mountaineer and the "wickedest" man alive – the occult legend Aleister Crowley.

Kabbalah was a vital thread running through the ceremonial magic of the Golden Dawn, a key that pulled all the philosophy together and gave it structure. The most common spelling used by the Golden Dawn and its pupils was *Qabalah*, and it is still usual to see western occultists use this spelling. The Hermetic Order of the Golden Dawn was structured much like a Rosicrucian mystery lodge,

many of their rituals and teachings. His reliability is somewhat uncertain – Crowley was an inveterate joker and prankster – but his material was extensive and plausible. Eventually, the entire Golden Dawn corpus was compiled into a book by the noted author and alumnus Israel Regardie, *The Complete Golden Dawn System of Magic*.

The Golden Dawn initiates produced a number of Kabbalistic works between them, most of which are still popular with western magicians today. These include Crowley's famous *Liber 777* (which is basically just a set of tables of correspondences), Regardie's *Garden of Pomegranates*, A. E. Waite's *Holy Kabbalah*, and Dion Fortune's *Mystical Qabalah*. In the years that have followed, western occult thinkers have welded Kabbalism almost seamlessly into modern mysticism and magic. Its assumptions and doctrines are now an unalienable part of our occult tradition.

LEFT: **Nineteenth-century France – Levi's influence is felt with this advert for a book of spiritualism and Rosicrucian magic.**

RIGHT: **The Egyptian god Harpocrates demonstrating his famous Sign of Silence, used in the Golden Dawn to close energy links after meditation.**

The Tree of Life

The Tree of Life (or *Otz Chiim*) is the master key for the gates of creation. The greatest of the Kabbalah's mysteries, it is the blueprint that underlies everything from the structure of the universe right down to the way the human personality is constructed. It is a model of the fractal building block of reality – God's route for approaching the world, and therefore our route for approaching God. It encompasses everything, structuring every aspect of reality within its complexities.

The Spark of Divinity

The doctrine of the Sundering expresses all of reality as an aspect of God's divided self, seeking reunification with divinity, connected to itself at all levels. This is remarkably similar to recent theories of quantum mechanics, which suggest that every subatomic particle is connected to every other one, and that each part contains the whole – the "holographic universe." Science and the Kabbalah say the same thing: that all was one, and then it split and became the universe, but remained connected, and will one day return to being one again.

The Tree of Life shows how the spark of divinity became the substance of the universe. It is the route from energy to matter, from God to Man. It is at the heart of each mote of existence, and so manifests time and again, in all areas, at all levels. Therefore, it is also a depiction of God himself: "as above, so below." Fractal mathematics show us that the shape of a leaf's pores echoes the shape of the leaf, and also the shape of the branch, and even the shape of the tree – so the Tree of Life can be found on all scales of reality, from the universal to the most personal.

The mystical and philosophical implications of the macrocosm and microcosm are advanced, and difficult to grasp. We work by comparisons and dualities, so it is hard for us to make sense of a scheme that talks about universal unity. For all practical purposes, it is enough to just know that the Tree of Life represents and explains

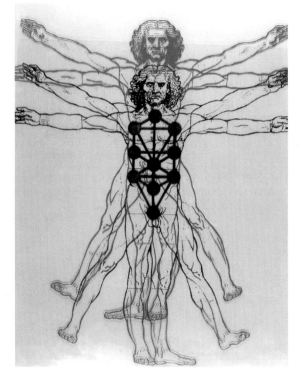

ABOVE: **As above, so below: an esoteric depiction shows the macrocosm as unified with the Tree of Life.**

RIGHT: **Adam Kadmon, the alchemists' archetypal man, is seen as the extrusion of the bottom seven Sephiroth of the Tree of Life in this illustration by Von Rosenroth.**

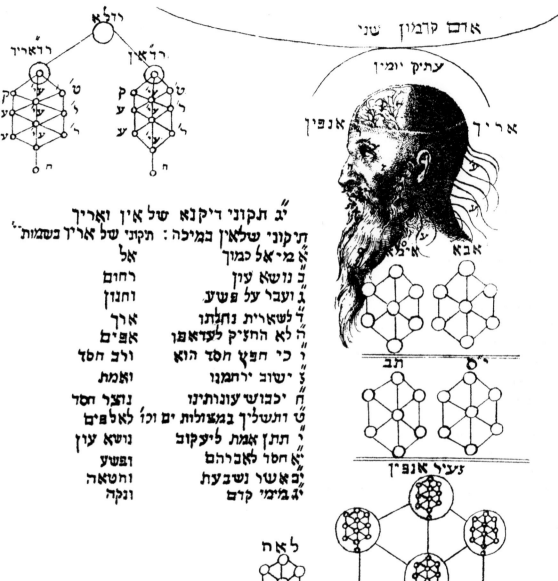

אדם קדמון שני

עתיק יומין

אריך אנפין

אבא אימא

רדלא
רדאיך רדאין

"יג תקוני דיקנא של אין ואריך
תיקוני שלאין במיכה : תקוני של אריך בשמות"

אל	"א מי אל כמוך
רחום	"ב נושא עון
וחנון	"ג ועבר על פשע
ארך	"ד לשארית נחלתו
אפים	"ה לא החזיק לעד אפו
ורב חסד	"ו כי חפץ חסד הוא
ואמת	"ז ישוב ירחמנו
נוצר חסד	"ח יכבוש עונותינו
נושא עון	"ט ותשליך במצולות ים וכו' לאלפים
ופשע	"י תתן אמת ליעקב
וחטאה	"יא חסד לאברהם
ונקה	"יב אשר נשבעת
	"יג מימי קדם

צעיר אנפין

לאה

יעקב

קליפות

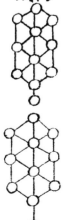

בריאה

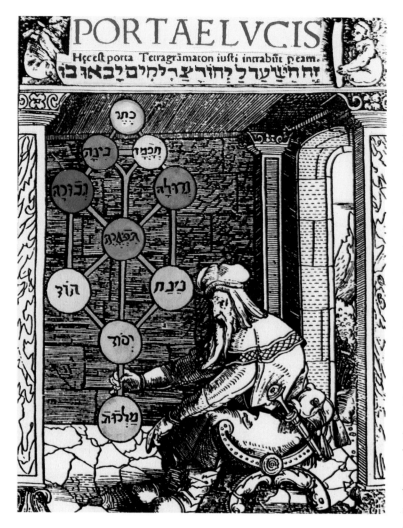

LEFT: **An early version of the Tree of Life is depicted with just sixteen paths connecting the ten Sephiroth.**

They are guides and channels rather than influences in their own right, and so their effects and natures are subtler, but it is a critical mistake to think that they are not significant in their own right. As the *Sepher Yetzirah* says, the Sephiroth and Nativoth together are the "thirty-two wondrous paths of wisdom engraved by God" in creating the universe.

When we have familiarized ourselves with the basic structure of the Tree, we will turn to explore some of its internal symbolism. Its deeper mysteries include the three pillars of the law, the veils of the limitless light, the four worlds of creation, the abyss (gateway to the "Dark Tree" of the *Qliphoth*), and the seven planes of existence. Each of these elements – even the most negative ones – can help to shed some light on the nature of the

many different levels of reality, and that all are linked. The teachings and exercises that the Sephiroth offer are not restricted to the transcendentally enlightened.

Over the course of this chapter, we are going to explore the Tree of Life in detail. First, we will look at each of the Sephiroth in turn. Each sphere represents one of the core qualities and principles from which the universe is built. They affect us on a myriad of levels, and offer a whole range of lessons and teachings. Just gaining some familiarity with the Sephiroth is enough to bring about a better understanding of life and the design of the universe.

Once we've examined the Sephiroth, we will look at the Nativoth, the paths of the Tree. They are the struts that interlink the spheres, providing conduits by which the forces of the Sephiroth can balance and interweave.

universe and what it means to be human.

Finally, before we begin, it is worth noting that there is still a certain amount of debate regarding the Tree of Life, just as there is in every other aspect of the Kabbalah. Various scholars have presented other schemes for structuring the Tree that vary in greater or lesser degrees. The variants can be thought of as different points of view: you can describe a wolf as a grey dog-like predator, a thickly-furred mammal, a frightening pack-hunter, or a member of the species *Canis lupus* without ever being inaccurate, and without ever quite expressing the totality. Similarly, the Otz Chiim is richer and more multi-textured than any one attempt to describe it or envision it. In this chapter, we will concentrate on the version of the Tree that is the most familiar and most widely studied and accepted.

The Structure of the Tree of Life

The Otz Chiim is an extremely profound and versatile symbol, with ties and links to a myriad of systems, and all sorts of internal representations and schemas. Before investigating its deeper mysteries, it is vital to have at least a basic understanding of the structure underlying it all.

On a purely superficial level, it is perhaps easiest to think of the Tree of Life as a map. It describes the route that the divine energy of God's sundered self uses to find expression in the physical world. By winding its way down from one Sephira to the next, the energy gains texture and meaning. Eventually, it is grounded into reality and takes its allotted form. The shards of the Sundering

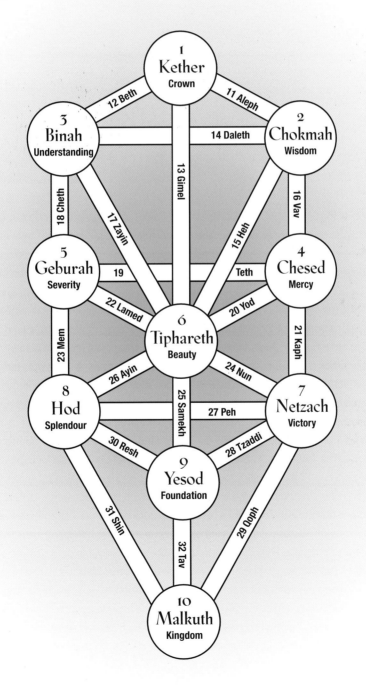

become all the aspects of the physical world – inanimate matter, human consciousness, physical actions, even intangible ideas. The Tree can illustrate any and all of these end results and encompasses all possibilities.

Before the existence of the Tree, there is just the infinity of God's divine light. Nothing else exists. The light is not generally thought to be the entirety of God himself, but it is his essence. In accordance with God's will and the Sundering, the light becomes conscious. This is the first Sephira of the Tree – *Kether*, the Crown. Set in the limitless light, Kether awakens to its own existence.

Despite its consciousness, Kether has no awareness. It is still undifferentiated – an infinite point, a unity that permits no externalization. The second Sephira, *Chokmah* (Wisdom) forms in response to Kether's unity. Chokmah is able to look back at Kether and perceive the wonder of the divine love. Two points provide the basis for a path, and the energy of the Sundering cascades down that path. Chokmah is both the source and recipient of that energy, and broadcasts it out joyfully.

A straight line gives scope for polarity, but not motion. The energy flooding out from Chokmah travels an infinite distance – but the universe of expression is curved back on itself. Eventually the energy returns to the point it originated from, back at Chokmah, while still travelling in a straight line. The limitless light is filled with Chokmah's energy, but the curve that the energy has been around describes an infinite blackness. This blackness becomes the third Sephira: *Binah*, Understanding, the womb of God. With Binah's formation, movement and space become meaningful. The new sphere receives Chokmah's infinite energy, mother to Chokmah's fatherhood.

Now that there are three points of reference in the limitless light, it is possible to begin to map out areas, to give distance and direction to energy. Binah organizes the energy of Chokmah, and divides it into quanta – the individual shards. All are still part of the whole, and Binah's oceans are very much still one whole, but there is also a sense that it is possible for subdivisions to exist. Having organized the divine energy, Binah emits it again, into the infinities it encompasses – a new direction. Finally the three dimensions of space are complete, and the real universe comes into being with the creation of the fourth sphere: *Chesed*, Mercy. In Chesed, the shards from Binah are clothed in all of the infinite variety of form that three dimensions of space allows for. Chesed is constant change and plenty without discrimination; perfect inclusiveness. Everything is welcome within Chesed, for there is no idea of shortage or foreignness.

The undiscriminating bounty· of Chesed causes

LEFT: **All is Light: the divine limit-less light of God is the wellspring from which all else comes into being.**

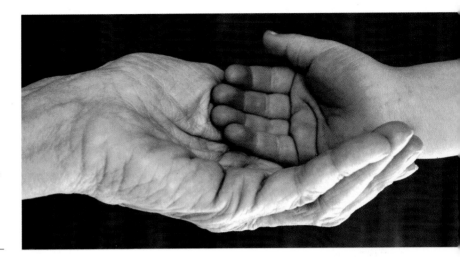

RIGHT: **All Sephiroth exist as manifest in our world of formation. *Chesed*, Mercy, can express itself through something as simple as a child's touch.**

problems, however. Not everything is meant to exist; there is not room for infinite amounts of everything possible. That brings up the requirement for some hard decisions. The fifth Sephira is *Geburah*, Severity. In its infinite love, Geburah understands that some elements must be sacrificed to make way for others more appropriate, necessary or successful. That which is not needed is slashed away, so that the whole may take its most perfect form.

That perfect form is manifested in the sixth Sephira: *Tiphareth*, Beauty. This is the City of Gold, home of the individual soul. It is the pinnacle of refinement, but it still reflects the perfection and beauty of the divine in all its wisdom. Tiphareth does not yet have any impetus for action, and without action, there can be no exploration. The perfection of Tiphareth, perceiving the need for motion, gives birth to the seventh Sephira: *Netzach*, Victory. Netzach is an engine of energy and direction. It is powered by the limitless energy of divinity, and seeks restlessly to provide the motion that Tiphareth requires. This motion is both physical and spiritual, and gives rise to emotion, the force that drives the personality.

Motion without direction however is self-defeating. To balance its energy, Netzach's need seeks dispassionate intelligence – *Hod*, Glory, the eighth Sephira. In Hod, Netzach's energy is analyzed, examined and given purpose. This is the place of rational thought and scrutiny, where communication becomes possible because the personal mind is taking shape. Drawing on the power of Netzach to drive it, Hod pushes its energies down into

Yesod, the Foundation, the ninth sphere. In Yesod, the glory of Tiphareth is reflected and mingled with the thought of Hod and the feeling of Netzach into a great melting pot of possibility. Splendours and nightmares exist here, in the realm of the imagination and unconscious. Yesod encompasses all that may be, all that was and all that can be envisaged.

Yesod is a murky and impure mirror, however. The true image of the divine cannot be allowed to manifest purely in the universe, for it would be a beacon to all of the shards of God's self, sweeping all individuality and free will away. For the Sundering to have meaning – for the shards of God to be able to experience – then the glory of Tiphareth must be hidden, at least a little. The manifest world cannot bear the light of God's perfection. Therefore, Yesod provides a filter between the rest of the Tree and the final Sephira: *Malkuth*, the Kingdom.

In Malkuth, Hod and Netzach are able to reach down to organize the energies of the divine – and the bounty of Chesed and Binah – into the patterns that lie beneath reality. These patterns are slotted into place within Malkuth, which then works with the primal forces to bring the world of matter into being. By coming into existence, Malkuth creates the universe, and the purpose of the Tree is finally realized and completed.

Now that we've looked at the Tree as a general overview, we will examine some of the implications of each of the spheres and paths. We shall start where all of us begin – in the Kingdom of God.

Malkuth, the Kingdom

Resplendent Intelligence: "God said: 'Be fruitful and multiply'"

TH   V   K   L   M

The tenth sphere, Malkuth (pronounced marl-KOOT) is the base of the Tree of Life, the lowest of all the Sephiroth. It is also known as *Shekhinah*, a term that refers to the female aspect of God – God the Mother, rather than the Father. As the Kingdom (or, perhaps more appropriately, "Queendom") Malkuth represents the state of being. It is stability, the end result, physical embodiment – the very end of the act of creation. As such, it is associated with mundane physical reality, finished products and end results, the fruits of any act of creation.

Personal consciousness and the interaction of the senses with the physical universe all fall within the realm of Malkuth. Its planetary symbol is the Earth, but it is important to note that the sphere is not the physical universe itself. Solid matter – reality – is the product of all ten spheres and 22 paths, rather than just one. Malkuth then is not reality as such, but it is the portal through which reality is given form; the mother, rather than the child.

In terms of the soul's journey and the development of the psyche, Malkuth is the realm of direct physical experience, the place where our senses interact with that which is real. Thought, emotion, memory and evocation have no place here – if you caress a piece of silk, Malkuth is the plain sensation of sheer softness, rather than any pleasure it evokes. It is sight and taste and touch devoid of context or analysis, experience without meaning. There is nothing really self-aware about Malkuth; alone and uncombined with other spheres, it is bestial and purposeless. Pure Malkuth has no emotion or reason, no mind to speak of; just a certain amount of instinct and reflex. In Malkuth, existence happens from moment to moment, free of context or meaning. There is just physical

LEFT: **Meadowsweet is said to be a powerful pain reliever and is associated in herb lore with love, divination, happiness and peace.**

RIGHT: **Rabbits are famed for their "sociable" lifestyles, embodying the physicality and fecundity of Malkuth.**

sensation and the awareness of it. As such, it is very close to the Greek concept of Hades, the hellish domain of empty shells.

This is not a bad thing, however. Without a solid, objective base for experience, there can be no reality. We all create our own meaning and significance internally for each event, and if we did not share a common base free of all assumptions, we could have no grounds for free-willed communication or existence. By remaining free of all emotion, thought and analysis, Malkuth ensures that it carries with it no assumptions. There is no built-in static to interfere with the way we create our view of reality. We have ultimate free will to determine our interactions with the world and each other – there is no dogma built in to Malkuth, no insistence on meanings or ethics or anything else. We are all individual, and by remaining entirely within the area of sensation, Malkuth allows us to share a world without compromising that individu-ality. For this reason, Malkuth is often referred to as the flower of the Tree of Life – we take the beauty from it that we seek.

On a more mystical level, Malkuth is the focus point for the rest of the forces of the Tree of Life. The Sephiroth express themselves into the world through Malkuth; it is a vital gateway, the first portal between the universe and the paths back to God – the gate to the orchard. Before the soul can start to seek its return to God, it first has to fully become separated, so Malkuth is the marker which denotes the point at which separation occurs – one has to pass beyond it before one can go back. As a balance point between physical matter and the energies of the spirit, it seethes with dynamic energies. Each Sephira is an infinity in it own right, and Malkuth is the infinity of boundless space speckled with tiny particles of matter.

Malkuth is often associated with the four classical elements of Greek philosophy: fire, air, water and earth. The elements themselves are further considered to represent energy, gasses, liquids and solids; power, will, intuition and strength; and destiny, spirit, life and inanimate matter. Malkuth is therefore usually depicted as the Cross of Equated Forces, divided into four equal quarters, coloured russet, citrine, olive and

black. As the only sphere of the Tree grounded into physical reality, Malkuth is the only stable Sephira – changing it takes time and effort, due sacrifices to the inertia of causality.

The lessons that Malkuth asks us to learn are focused on operating within the real world. We exist, as humans, in a sea of relationships that we share with other humans. Can we learn to apply the wisdoms we acquire in other areas of the Tree to our lives as social animals? Can we learn to cherish the senses and let go of the static that we associate with them? Can we appreciate moments of peace, beauty and love for what they are? These are the challenges of the sphere of Malkuth.

When visualizing Malkuth, it is usually depicted as a four-quartered Temple in an underground cavern,

representing its position as the foundation of the four elements that make up the world. A long, rough tunnel some ten feet high winds its way through dark rock, lit by burning wooden torches. The tunnel is drafty, and the stone is damp, even wet in places, but the air is not cold. After a time, the tunnel leads to a set of stairs carved into the rock. They lead through a circular hole in the roof. Climbing the steps leads to the Temple of Equated Forces, a square cavern carved smoothly out of the rock and floored with sparkling sheets of marble. Each wall is covered by a curtain of shimmering silk. A stone altar stands in front of each curtain, holding a plain candle. Straight ahead from the point of entry – to the east – the curtain and candle are sky blue, and represent Raphael, the archangel of air. Behind, they are pure white, and represent Gabriel, archangel of water. To the right, they are bright red, and represent Michael, archangel of fire. Finally, to the left, they are a rich gold, and represent Uriel, archangel of earth.

Malkuth is also associated with the colour sky blue, gates, the human body, sandalwood, clover, oak trees, rock crystal, the magic circle, rabbits, gnomes, the virtue of discrimination, Mother Earth, organizational techniques and the moment of birth.

BELOW: **Malkuth, as the gateway through which the universe manifests, is astronomically associated with the planet Earth, cradle of our lives.**

Yesod, Foundation

Pure Intelligence: "God said: 'Let us make man'"

ד ו ס י

D   V   S   Y

The ninth sphere, Yesod (pronounced yeŘ-SODD) means "Foundation," and is the first sphere that Malkuth connects to, the place of interface between the state of just being and the wisdom represented by the rest of the Tree. It is also known as *Tzaddik*, which means "righteousness." Yesod is described as the "pure" intelligence because it is the final product of the rest of the Tree, just prior to its ultimate embodiment into the chaos of the world through Malkuth.

To understand Yesod, it is necessary to look at its position on the Tree. The sphere is often identified with the moon, and like the moon, it reflects the light of the sun/soul from its home in Sephira 6, Tiphareth, straight down to the earth/body, in Malkuth. It is also connected to the spheres of thought and feeling (Netzach and Hod, 7 and 8 respectively), but it lies below their level, close to the unthinking instinct of Malkuth.

In other words, Yesod is the sphere of the unconscious. It integrates the past with the urgings and tendencies of the higher soul, and blends that material in with conscious thought and feeling, feeding the resultant material to the self. This is a realm of the imagination and the unconscious, of phantoms, dreams, legends and horrors. Self-awareness begins here, in the dim memories of past pains and glories, and the inherited needs of the soul.

Yesod receives all of the urges and imaginings generated within Malkuth. It is a sphere of illusions and phantasms, as infinitely malleable as Malkuth is stubbornly inflexible. The past lives on here, in patterns cast by prior events and thoughts – not just individually, but collectively as well, for after all, we are all one. When you look into your mind's eye and work with your imagi-

nation, you are manipulating the stuff of Yesod. When you dream, this is the sphere that you wander through. Yesod is a place of unbridled creativity, where anything can be brought into existence and given a chance to show itself. This is the realm of the psychic and the astral – a place of possibilities rather than truths.

Without the influence of Yesod, there would be no house for the influence of the past, no place for common understanding, no way for the light of the divine to touch the world. Formation takes place here; patterns filter down to Yesod from the rest of the Tree and are turned into blueprints by which Malkuth can bring them into manifestation. All that is and was lives on in Yesod's reflections. This is the home of symbolism, hidden meanings and desires, and all manner of images and chimeras. It is the path by which the divine light of the soul is able to make itself manifest within the world. If it shone directly onto Malkuth, the beauty of Tiphareth, the pure house of the soul, would sweep away our free will in a bright burst of divine love. Every soul yearns for completeness, for the return first to Tiphareth, and then up to Kether, unity with God, but if that completion were enforced, there would be no room for growth or understanding – it would be as if God had never sundered himself in the first place.

So, by acting as a confused, misty mirror for the glories of the soul in Tiphareth – as well as the fires of the mind in Hod and the waves of emotion in Netzach – Yesod allows Malkuth, with all its imperfections, to remain in existence. Without it, the entire universe would be swept back up in the rapture that is Kether, oneness with God. Yesod is a dark, twisted mirror, but it has to be, because the light that it reflects is so intense.

Be aware though that like any other mirror, Yesod reflects both ways, and while it does distort the glory of the divine, it also purifies the physical. Illusions can not pass upwards out of Yesod. Furthermore, like a more conventional mirror, it brings the soul into the personality

through the unconscious, but it can also show twisted aspects of the personality back to itself. Horrors and glories can be generated out of the twists in our own unconscious. Yesod is a dangerous sphere: a trap for illusions, both our own and others', layered over the years. We need to learn to identify our own fantasies (both good and bad) before we can move through Yesod in safety. Many mystics have been trapped here by false wonders and terrors.

Are you able to tell the difference between a twisted reflection of your own fears and desires, and a true reflec-tion of your divine will? Are you ready to look beyond the words and tricks of false prophets and see the beauty of God's light? These are the challenges that you will need to rise to in order to master the many nodes of Yesod.

In meditations, Yesod is normally visualized as a grassy hilltop clearing poking out of a vast forest of trees. The forest is full of hidden, distant activity. It is night, and the moon is overhead, its phase corresponding to the current physical one. The only colour is a dark indigo wash over the blacks, whites and greys of the scene – and even then, only when the moon is at least half full. Toward the

ABOVE LEFT: **Seen as guardians of the underworld and consummate tricksters in many cultures, cats are strongly linked with Yesod.**

ABOVE: **Said to soothe and bring peace and sleep, lavender is associated with Yesod's hidden depths.**

centre of the clearing, a wide circle of stones surrounds a ring of pillars. Each stone is about a foot round, half white and half black. The pillars themselves come in pairs, one black and one white. At the top, exactly level with your face, each pair holds a round mirror. There are nine pairs, distributed evenly around the circle. As you stand at the centre and look into the mirrors, you see that each contains a different aspect of your personality; positively skewed, negatively skewed and undistorted versions of your childish ego, your restrictive, parental id, and your rational "true self."

Yesod is variously associated with the colour indigo, mirrors, the sexual organs, lavender, violets, willow trees, incense, cats, vampires, the virtue of independence, burial mounds, employee rights and the moment of conception.

Hod, Glory

Perfect Intelligence: "God said: 'Let the earth bring forth living creatures'"

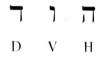

D   V   H

The eighth sphere, Hod (pronounced HORD) means "Glory", but is also variously translated as splendour, majesty, brightness and beauty. It is at the base of the left-hand column of the Tree, known as the pillar of severity. Hod represents the glory of the kingdom of Earth as perceived by the rational mind. All is consistent here, ordered and catalogued, put and kept in place – this is an oasis of reason among the ever-shifting sand dunes of chaotic reality.

Hod is linked to the planet Mercury, and forms the centre of analysis, communication and systems within the Tree. This is where form is expressed in terms that relate to objective reality. Psychologists have known for some time that the human mind perceives and analyzes by comparisons and differences. We identify things, literally, by what they are not, fitting them into boxes. The number "3" is bigger than "2" and smaller than "4", so we know to put it between them in sequence. Similarly, each time we look at an object, a complex

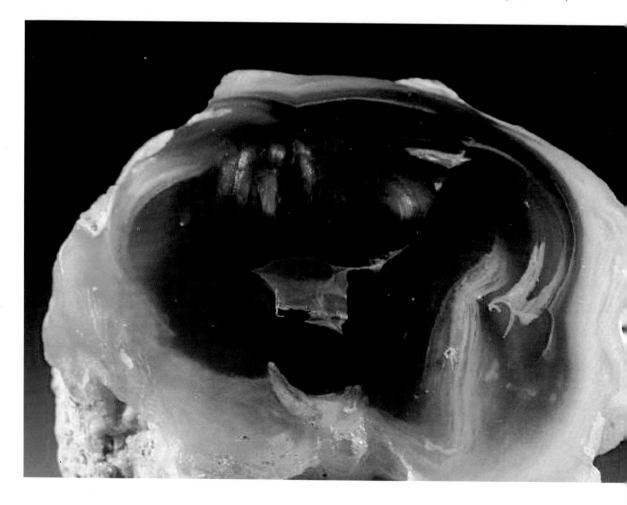

cascade of analyses takes place – shutting off options of colour, shape, size, texture and so on until we come to a point where there are no other comparisons to be made, and we have identified the item. Similarly, when we are choosing rational paths of action, we evaluate and compare outcomes, and select the most desirable; and so on, right through the mind.

This processing is the province of Hod. This is the first place where we become truly conscious, able to differentiate ourselves from the rest of the world by knowing what is us and what is not. As humans, our sense of conscious awareness is split across the triangle

BELOW: **According to folklore, the fox is the most cunning of all the animals, embodying the spirit of Hod.**

LEFT: **Fire opal, the gemstone associated with Hod, is said to promote spontaneous action, stimulate new ideas and generate enthusiasm.**

of Hod, Netzach (feeling), and Malkuth. Our personality lies inside and beneath this triangle, in the unconscious depths of Yesod. Within Hod, we are able to process, discriminate, compartmentalize and analyze. It is sometimes said that in Hod, we take individual thoughts and notions and wall them off in prisons of flame, separate, segregated and impenetrable.

Like all three pairs of Sephiroth, Hod requires balance with Netzach to remain a healthy influence. Hod is all about organization and direction. The universe is full of intricate complexities and subtleties. All the diversity of pure chaos is structured by rational intelligence into infinitely flexible systems – and we retain the ability to observe, analyze and work with even the most complex things, thanks to our powers of abstraction and symbolism. This ability to catalogue and identify – to rationalize – allows us to work with and express our desires and creativity. Before we can produce an end result, we have to have the emotion driving us to achieve it, and the mind directing that desire into a blueprint. At that point, expression becomes meaningfully possible.

Without Hod's constant work to separate and identify, there would be no way of meaningfully understanding anything. We need our myriad of different mental tokens to be able to communicate with one another, to provide a basis for action, to be able to learn and develop. Yesod may contain and reflect the past, but in Hod, its legacy lives on in the structures and patterns of our rational minds.

The danger of all of this, of course, is that Hod is prone to control, and it must be balanced with the fluidity of Netzach. Force needs to be directed, but if there are too many blocks and controls in the channels, the force is dissipated before it can do anything, and the form becomes stagnant. Hod demands that you think and analyze, but that you do so from a position where you are in touch with your emotional desires. Control without compassion is tyranny. Are you able to make rational decisions that incorporate your needs and emotions? Do you know when to analyze, and when to act? Can you see the truth in among the information? These are the questions posed to you by Hod.

In meditations, Hod is pictured as a vast, complicated library at the heart of a bustling desert trade-town. Nomads, merchants and caravan trains are constantly streaming in and out of the town by all five of its trade routes. Inside the library, the main chamber is a huge, eight-sided vault six stories tall. Upper stories are accessed by a central staircase. A dozen archways lead off each level, separated by tall cases crammed full of books, scrolls and manuscripts. Each archway (and bookcase) corresponds to one of the 72 letters of the true name of God, which describes all creation, and leads to another chamber. Some of the secondary chambers are comparatively small, while others snake off along series of vaults and passageways and catacombs that can lead on for miles. All human thought is collected within the books of the library. The library is usually busy with other students, assorted teachers and masters of certain areas of knowledge, and even librarians who can help provide guidance and direction – although on some occasions, particularly early on, it may appear to be empty and confusing. Note that the library does not specialize in facts or historical matter, except as such things relate to rational analysis and debate. Stating a need, following intuitive guidance to a specific spot and book, and then picking up the book and reading (or talking to others pictured at that location) can yield some very interesting insights.

Hod is usually associated with the colour orange, books, the kidneys, rosemary, pansies, hazel trees, fire opal, spells, foxes, elves, the virtue of truthfulness, man-made structures, business processes and moments of understanding.

RIGHT: **True verbena, also known as vervain, is a long-standing folk remedy for depression and a range of nervous disorders.**

Netzach, Victory

Hidden Intelligence: "God said: 'Let the waters swarm'"

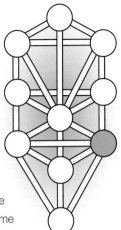

ת צ נ

Ch   Tz   N

The seventh sphere, Netzach (pronounced NET-zarck) means "Victory," but is also variously translated as endurance, faithfulness, permanence, eternity, excellence, completion and perfection. It sits opposite and before Hod, at the base of the right-hand column of the Tree, the pillar of mercy, and is linked with the planet Venus. Note that Netzach is a polar complement and opposite to Hod; it cannot ever be really understood rationally, just intuitively and emotionally. By definition, any rational understanding of Netzach is at least partially distorted by the workings of Hod.

In terms of human experience, Netzach is the source and home of the feelings. Just as Hod is the home of thought rather than of specific facts, so Netzach embodies the higher feelings, rather than any particular emotion – individual emotions are produced along the path of Tzaddi, which connects Netzach to Yesod. This sphere delights in dreams, free

from fears or confusions; it is laden with emotional wealth, supported obediently by reason, imagination and sensation. It is immediate, illogical and spontaneous; an emotional gut response that the personality then takes and shapes into our own individual primary response. It ignites the rational, giving it the power to take action, but is itself entirely pre-rational. By the time we can analyze it and name it as an emotion, the spark itself has already flashed through. Netzach is not a sphere for words.

There is none of the divisive analysis of rationality at this point in the Tree. Netzach is the pure emanation of spirituality, unsullied by discrimination, unconscious urges or the demands of the ego. It takes in the energy of the divine, filtered down through the Tree from Kether, and pushes out the ever-renewing force of life and growth. Netzach is the wellspring of the energy which is variously referred to as *Chi, Prana*, manna, the divine light, the Force, and so on. In fact, "force" is a particularly good word, because it is the power of Netzach, filtered through the purpose of Hod, which allows action and reaction. In its pure state, within its own Sephira, it has no form or direction.

Humans usually think of this pure emotional energy in terms of divine love, and indeed Netzach is strongly associated with the archetype of Venus. It is perhaps the easiest way for us to interpret the creative energy of the universe – the pure light of life-force. It is an infinitely deep point, a singularity that is both infinite in scope and vanishingly small. It contains no dimensions as such, because it does not contain the differentiation of Hod. As this energy expresses itself into human understanding, it starts to clothe itself in form: moving into the experience of Hod. At this point, on the boundaries of Netzach, the

energy becomes the archetypes of our human understanding of the higher emotions. Our understanding of love, as embodied among westerners by Venus, is one such archetype, but like any division or understanding of the whole, it is incomplete.

All the other mythological archetypes of familiar human expression can be found within Netzach too. At the edge of the Sephira, the undifferentiated force starts to take form. Note that negativity is introduced further down the Tree by human fears and jealousies, and the free will to block positivity. This means that the energies here are at their brightest. So, as the force of Netzach starts to become expressed, it takes on a myriad of shapes.

Within its own boundaries however, Netzach is the pure energy of life. Every act of creation draws on and through this sphere. It is the mystery of nature, the drive of all living things to be and grow. It is non-judgemental, because it does not seek to differentiate. It is goodness, because it finds no difference. It connects

us all, a collective wellspring of light and love that powers everything. However, it still requires Hod's assistance before its energy can be put to use. There needs to be an understanding of direction for motion to begin – and a direction implies one way in contrast to all other possible ways.

Hod and Netzach can only function together, and it is difficult to understand either without simultaneously considering the role of the other. Hod discriminates, but without Netzach, is has nothing to describe, no counterpoint with which to form its existence; Netzach drives, but without Hod, has no structure, and can achieve nothing. Order and chaos are both required for life to exist.

The creative spark, the mystery of life, the sheer joy of being alive: Netzach asks you to live in the moment, not bestially, as in Malkuth, but with the perfect appreciation of the love that makes up the universe. Can you surrender yourself to a moment of inspiration? Can you appreciate the mystery and wonder that is the universe, without trying to analyze or classify? These are the challenges that Netzach poses, and it is only possible to advance up the Tree to the next Sephira, the home of the

soul itself, if you are able to let go, and accept the joy on its own terms.

In meditations, Netzach is usually pictured as a lush, sunny countryside of attractive woodlands and flower-filled meadows. Babbling streams wind through the landscape. The scene is filled with harmonious living creatures going peacefully and playfully about their business. There is a deep sense of abiding joy and love here. On one sun-drenched slope, a gentle path of white chalk leads up to a circle of ivy-covered apple trees. There are seven trees, more or less evenly spaced. The ivy that grows on them winds from branch to branch and treetop to treetop, making it look as if all the trees are growing together into one ring. The grass inside the trees is thick and luxurious, free of nettles and thorns, and the sun shines down – perfect for stretching out. It is an idyllic spot, disturbed only by the occasional dove cooing.

Netzach is usually associated with the colour green, growing things, the solar plexus, patchouli, grass, apple trees, emerald, lamps, doves, fauns, the virtue of selflessness, natural landscape features, permission to act and moments of feeling.

LEFT: **Doves have long been considered to be symbols of love and peace – the association with Venus linking them to the power of Netzach.**

RIGHT: **Admired for their beauty, emeralds are known as the stone of successful love. They enhance understanding, draw love and open and clear the heart chakra.**

Tiphareth, Beauty

Mediating Intelligence: "God said: 'Let there be lights in the firmament'"

Th   R   A   P   Th

The sixth sphere, Tiphareth (pronounced tip-EH-rett) means "Beauty" and harmony, and is also sometimes known as *Rokhmim,* or Mercy. It is at the centre of the Tree of Life, the sacred heart of the entire scheme where the divinity of the upper Tree meets the worldliness of the lower. In Tiphareth, there are no enemies, for all are friends, long-parted and reunited in joy. The old are rejuvenated, wisdom intact; the young are encouraged to play and explore and grow. There is no call for fighting or selling. It is the jubilee, the summer fair, and all the scattered family have come home. Dreams and memories are reunited laughingly as advice and history, and there is an answer to each question. The desert and the pounding sea are united as a gentle, golden beach. This is the city of gold, the best of all places, where the immortal soul makes its home, away from the tribulations of its ventures into the physical world.

Tiphareth is associated with the sun, and the sphere is indeed radiant and expressive. It is a place of equilibrium, a dynamic balance between the universal spheres of the higher Tree and the more personal spheres of the inner self. All the forces of creation come into Tiphareth, and the joyous dance of weaving them all together requires constant attention. On a personal level, this is the work of the immortal soul. It is the focus point of the divine forces, the spark of "I" that has the attention and power to manifest the energy down through the Tree, accreting personality and physical existence so that it can experience life in the universe. It is driven by the Divine's need for self-realization expressed in the Sundering, and time and again it drives itself downward into incarnation, learning and evolving from each experience until it is fully aware.

In a more general sense, Tiphareth is the sun, the light that allows existence. The more abstract Sephiroth higher up the Tree are softened and mediated in Tiphareth, so that they can go on to provide the energies that manifestation in the universe requires without disrupting the flow of life itself. It is the ultimate middle-man, exposing the mundane to the light of the divine without scorching it away, whilst also allowing the divine to see itself through the mundane without becoming polluted. All must pass through Tiphareth. It is the source of the divine in life.

Note that the intelligence embodied in Tiphareth is particularly pure and dispassionate. It is the part of the mind that is listening when you talk to yourself, the "I" that

as the ultimate state of being to aspire toward. Within Tiphareth, there is no jealousy or petty spite, no pain or lust, no frustrated desire or compulsive striving – there is just compassion, peace and acceptance, enough for the whole world. By seeking to bring the personality more closely in line with the soul in Tiphareth, the mystic performs two important functions: one is to reduce the soul's workload in its dance of mediation, and the other is to increase the clarity of the connection between the self and the divine. With more time available to it, the soul itself has more opportunity for improvement and for bringing itself in turn closer to the true divinity of Kether's limitless light, which allows an even closer connection between the self and God.

ABOVE: **According to the traditional language of flowers, the yellow rose is a powerful symbol of joy and satisfaction.**

RIGHT: **Topaz is the soul stone. It transforms negativity into joy, boosts creativity and individuality, and helps the wearer see their own motivations and desires.**

is capable of being aware of the notion of self. Emotions, associations, needs and experiences all take place lower down the Tree, and the soul is free of these burdens. To experience the state of being of Tiphareth, one has to leave these accumulations behind. The personality is a product of Yesod, a shell that accumulates around the soul so that it can interact with the worlds of Malkuth, Hod and Netzach.

Most organized religions depict the ideals of Tiphareth

This is the true nature of the great work within the orchard. By working from within Malkuth to bring the lower spheres of the conscious personality into close alignment with the soul in Tiphareth, the Kabbalist is able to decrease the impurities and pollutants that get in the way of his or her experience of God. In the doctrine of the Sundering, all things and actions are part of God's efforts to know Himself, reflections of the divine. This spark is Tiphareth, and it is within everything.

To step aside from the personality entirely, and look objectively and lovingly at yourself and the world around you – this is the task that Tiphareth demands. Mastering this is usually considered the final prerequisite for achieving the enlightenment of unity with the divine, and it brings great personal peace and acceptance. Obviously, it is far from easy.

In meditations, Tiphareth is a large, sprawling city made of pure gold. All the buildings are built of gold bricks; the streets are paved with gold slabs. Edges, seams and decorations are picked out with perfect jewels, particularly diamonds. It is always midday, and the impact of the full sun shining onto the city should be utterly blinding, but somehow it is still possible to see. There are homes and market squares and golden gardens, and you are aware that all the calm, ageless people who throng the city are old, old friends. At the very heart of the city, right at the centre at the point of perfect equilibrium, is a beautiful 12-sided temple. Inside it, a gigantic diamond hangs in mid-air over the centre point. Each of its 400 facets radiates a brilliance brighter than anything our universe has to offer. A particularly intense beam of light shines down into a dark, six-sided hole in the floor – the light of the soul illuminating the personality of Yesod and life circumstances of Malkuth. A plain, functional-looking broadsword lies along one edge of the hole, representing the power of the self to direct its will in the here and now.

Tiphareth is associated with the colour gold, the home, the heart, rose, gorse, holly trees, topaz, altars, spiders, fairies, the virtue of devotion, stone circles, inspiration and moments of peace.

LEFT: **Like Tiphareth itself, the spider sits at the centre of its universe of connections, linked to the paths around it. Its presence brings the web to life.**

Geburah, Severity

Radical Intelligence: "God said: 'Let the earth put forth grass'"

ה ר ו ב ג

H   R   V   B   G

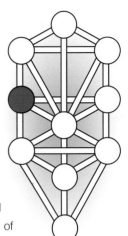

The fifth sphere, Geburah (pronounced gebb-oo-RAH) is usually taken to mean "Severity," although strength, might and power are all possible translations, and sometimes the English transliteration is written with a "v" rather than a "b" – Gevurah. The Sephira is also known as *Din*, which means law, and *Pakhad*, or fear. It sits at the middle of the left-hand column, above Tiphareth. Geburah is associated with the planet Mars, and shares the same red colour. It is the sphere of sacrifice, destruction and loss, and as such, it is one of the most important – and most fundamentally misunderstood – influences in the entire Tree.

Like the other paired Sephiroth – such as Hod and Netzach – Geburah is an influence that has to be balanced and tempered by its opposite number, *Chesed*. The two are at opposite ends of a spectrum, and either unchecked will create disaster. It is vital to keep this in mind whilst considering the nature of Geburah, because it is difficult for humanity to reconcile with its nature.

Geburah is the sphere of rational destruction. This is a place of tyranny and acceptable losses, of collateral damage and military intelligence, of harsh judgement and merciless will. Despite its inflexible ruthlessness, there is no malice or error in Geburah's work. It is not evil, in any sense of the word – utterly pragmatic and totally dedicated, yes, but never unnecessary or cruel. It is strong, but never malevolent.

The watchwords of Geburah are understanding, rationality and caution. Hard decisions are made and implemented here, for the good of the whole. That which can be saved will be saved, and the rest will be cut away with as little fuss as possible. It has the intense focus of a laser beam. It flenses and purifies, cutting away excess and anything that is unhealthy so that there is room for fresh,

healthy growth and development. That which has over-extended itself devours too much in the way of resources, diverting vital energy away from other, more important processes. Geburah is the sword that restores the balance.

This is a vital aspect of all natural processes. Periods of destruction stimulate new, better growth. The muscle-building process is a great example. During intensive exercise with heavy weights, the muscles are pushed beyond their capabilities. Nutrients and energy sources are burned up, toxic waste products are produced, and the muscles themselves are subject to little rips and tears in a whole multitude of locations. After the exercise is over, rest and assorted nutrients heal the tears with stronger tissue, longer-term stored energy is released (helping to remove excess body fat), and the toxic chemicals are flushed out of the system. The net result is that the muscles become stronger and healthier; without the periods of destruction through exercise, they waste away until they atrophy entirely. The same holds true for pruning dead wood off plants to stimulate new leaves and branches, or cutting diseased flesh away from a wound.

Sacrifice, another of Geburah's aspects, is often thought of as a pointless waste of something valuable, but that too is a negative misunderstanding. True sacrifice is about withdrawing energy from one thing or area so that more energy is available in other areas. You have to sacrifice a certain amount of your social life and free time to bring up children, because you have to reallocate some of your energies. Sacrifice is a rational transaction in which greater amounts of some desired thing are obtained by reducing the amounts of something which is desired less. If a relationship is failing, you can only make room and energy for a new, hopefully better one by sacrificing the comforts of the older one. Similarly, to go from being fat and unfit to slim and toned, involves

sacrifice of certain food types and a proportion of inactive time in order to make room for a new physique and lifestyle.

Geburah is not a sphere of rage or hatred. It is every bit as loving as Tiphareth, Netzach or any of the other Sephiroth. Its purpose is to help and heal through reduction. In attack, Geburah is passionately righteous and unswerving. It knows what has to be done, and it has the unflinching will to do it. The real evil would be to fall short, and to do less than what is needed. If just a fraction of a fraction can be saved, and all the rest must be sacrificed to preserve just that shard – and there is truly nothing else that can be done – then Geburah will make that sacrifice, without flinching.

We do not often realize it, for our world frequently preaches to us that gentle meekness is the highest moral ideal, but Geburah is one of our best, most honest friends within the Tree of Life. Kind, merciful obedience is the morality of the slave; the wise ruler knows that mercy and severity, Sephiroth 4 and 5, must be kept in balance, and the pair illuminated in the light of true understanding – Binah, Sephira 3, as we will see shortly. When nothing else will produce the greatest good, do you have the will to do what is required, no matter how distasteful? That is the challenge of Geburah, and few people ever manage to rise to it.

In meditations, Geburah is usually pictured as a solid five-sided fortress created out of ice and fire. Its walls are thick and plain, offering no weakness or showy ornamentation. It stands on a large outcrop of heavy red rock, dominating a landscape of shifting balefire, the raging energy of spiritual power unleashed. At the base of the outcrop, paths of similar rock pick their way through the balefire. Inside the heart of the fortress there is a large, five-sided hall paved in sheets of solid fire, inter-locked with thick veins of sparkling ice. A large iron pentacle is inlaid into the floor, linking each corner of the room to each other. The room's centre is dominated by a five-sided font of fire, and a long, heavy sword that sits at its base.

Geburah is associated with the colour red, swords, the adrenal glands, cypress, peonies, rowan trees, ruby, spears, horses, dwarves, the virtue of courage, judgement stones, challenging authority and moments of necessity.

Chesed, Mercy

Measuring Intelligence: "God said: 'Let the waters be gathered' "

ד ס ח

D S Ch

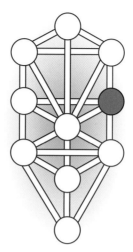

RIGHT: **Dolphins are famous for rescuing drowning sailors – an indication of the mercy and generosity of these highly intelligent creatures.**

The fourth sphere, Chesed (pronounced HESS-ed) is translated as "Mercy," and also denotes compassion and loving kindness. It is also known as *Gedulah*, which implies greatness, majesty and magnificence. It is the centre of the right-hand column, in balance with Geburah. Chesed is associated with the planet Jupiter, and is coloured blue. It is the sphere of perfect plenty, of growth, peace, abundance, acceptance and love.

Chesed's main quality is that of expansion. It is the first sphere, descending down the Tree, in which the concept of physical existence can be expressed, because four points of reference are required for three dimensions to take form. In Chesed, the divine love is finally able to take on shape and true existence. Its energies centre on growth; there is no lack or absence. This is an expansive place, where all is inclusive, linked – part of a sense of community and commonality. The primal force of loving kindness expresses itself by bringing together, assimilating and including and growing. It is far more powerful and fundamental than its complementary energy of repulsion and severance, as expressed by Geburah.

Another element of Chesed's growth and inclusion is that it brings constant development and change. The force of change is the way by which we tell one moment from the next, by which the future becomes the present and the present becomes the past. If there were no change, then there would be no time, and no growth. Chesed's loving inclusiveness manifests here, too. The near future is a direct expression of the present, and the present in turn is a direct expression of the recent past. Causality is a spectrum of threads, the ultimate inclusion.

To be within Chesed is to experience perfect peace and love. There is ultimate acceptance of all that comes. There is no fear, because Chesed understands that all

is one, and that the divine is immortal and unchanging. In its love, all anxiety and desire are set aside. By surrendering all fears and longings and plans, it becomes possible to control the moment. This is the power to do anything that is desired – but when one is free of fear and longing, nothing is desired. There is great power in love and acceptance, greater than will and destruction can ever attain, but there is also no impetus for its use. To achieve the power of Chesed is to understand that there is no need to apply it. This mystery is at the heart of Zen Buddhism, and all other paths to enlightenment. When all is said and done, the purpose of God's Sundering is understanding and experience, not competition or amassing the greatest notional score.

As the Sephira of growth, change and actualization, Chesed is the source of archetypal ideas, where the blueprints of creation first begin to take on some level of actuality. Potentials and end results are first imagined here. Sculptors and artists work with this energy when they are first beginning the creative process, as do all others who regularly have to imagine a new complete object or process before it has been begun. Chesed brims with all the things that have been conceived, without judgement or favour. Change and growth go hand in hand with novelty and innovation.

This is one of the reasons that Geburah and Chesed are so vital to each other. Without objective, unsentimental judgement and the associated destruction of that which hinders or eats up unwarranted resources, the Tree of

Life would choke and stifle on Chesed's generous, all-inclusive nature. However, Chesed comes before Geburah on the Tree of Life, and so the energy that passes to Geburah comes to it straight from Chesed's kind, loving mercy. This gives Geburah the necessary understanding to do its work as compassionately as its nature allows, preventing the possible evils that might result from imbalance of will.

When approaching Chesed, the Kabbalist is asked to put aside the fears and desires that the illusion of individuality breeds, and to remember that we are all one, part of the spark of the divine. By remembering that one is

all and all is divine love, infinite compassion, mercy and acceptance become possible. Chesed challenges the seeker to love without reserve, regardless of everything else. If you can contemplate the act of holding ultimate power without any temptation to change anything, then you have understood the lesson that Chesed has to teach.

When visualized, Chesed is generally imagined as a peaceful, luxurious town surrounded by rolling farmland. Golden wheat-fields nestle next to fruit-laden orchards, vegetable gardens, vineyards and all sorts of other crops. Well-travelled roads wind away into the distance. The town itself is bustling happily. Craft-houses and bakeries alternate with small businesses of all kinds. Nothing is for sale; all is available to those who need it. Everyone is content, healthy and happy, a vital and satisfied part of the community. Storehouses all through the town are overflowing with goods of all sorts, including items which might seem anachronistic in the setting – all that you could desire, free for you to take. The thought awakens no greed, just a deep-seated sense of peace and right-ness. At the centre of the town, a beautiful square holds a small temple in the form of four marble columns arranged in a square. Arches of water spout out of the top of each column, meeting at the centre of the temple. Soft, refreshing rain tinkles down from that point, filling the temple. At ground level, a fountain spouts from the middle of a small, square patch of beautiful flowers. At head-height, where the fountain peaks and splits to rain back down on the ground, a large, beautiful diamond hangs in the air. It is surrounded by mist from the rain and the fountain, and it shines with a wondrous light, which the mists soften into a gorgeous set of rainbow rings.

Chesed is associated with the colour blue, crop fields, the shoulders, cedarwood, tulips, birch trees, sapphire, wands, dolphins, sphinxes, the virtue of alignment, festival sites, corporate dialogue and moments of innovation.

LEFT: **From its position on the plains of Gizeh, the Sphinx majestically oversaw the fertile region of the Nile delta.**

BELOW: **Tulips originally grew wild in Persia, where they were said to arise from the spilled blood of a lover. It is said to be a generous, firm flower.**

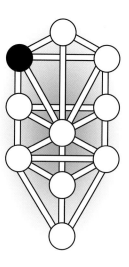

Binah, Understanding

Sanctifying Intelligence: "God said: 'Let there be a firmament'"

H   N   I   B

The third sphere, Binah (pronounced bee-NAR) is translated as "Understanding." It is also sometimes known as *Marah*, the great sea. Binah is associated with the planet Saturn, and is coloured black. It is the sphere of spiritual awareness, completion and division, and the vision of the valley of sorrows. This is the place where the divine energy is chopped into pieces, ready to take individual form in Chesed.

Binah is inseparably linked with the two earlier spheres – *Chokmah* (Intelligence) and *Kether* (Crown) – as a trinity of influences that are primarily divine in their nature, existing on pre-rational levels. These three, known as the supernal triad, are very hard for humanity to truly imagine or connect with, because they exist on a level more primal even than that of our immortal essence – they are the realm of the truly undifferentiated, the all-in-one. There is no duality within the supernal triad; everything here contains its own duality, becoming inherently self-contradictory. Naturally this makes the higher spheres difficult to discuss and explain, because their essences are pre-rational. Binah is the first sphere that has much in the way of meaning that makes sense to a human mind.

As an inherently dual or self-contradictory energy – and, what's more, one that is facing the rational portion of the Tree – Binah is often said to have two faces. The first is the point where Binah links to the Nativoth *Zayin* and *Chet*, the paths from Tiphareth and Geburah. It is the part of Binah most clearly visible to those of us resident in the lower portion of the Tree and looking up – the crone, the dark, sterile mother. After the lavish beauty of Chesed, Binah is a barren wasteland. There is no differentiation in this sphere, so there is nothing within it but the sphere

RIGHT: **Saturn is the planet of wisdom and mature understanding. Just as it represents the very different star signs of Capricorn and Aquarius, it also embodies Binah's duality of restriction and creation.**

itself. No wealth, no bounty, no life, no light, just endless blackness. As the head of the pillar of severity, it is easy to mistake Binah from the position of the outsider. Looking up the Tree, it is a frightening and forbidding place.

Worse, to arrive in Binah is to be stripped of all that makes you who you are. With no differentiation at all, there is no sense of self, no change, no time. Although the personality has long since been left behind in Hod and Netzach, individuality remains all the way through Tiphareth, Geburah and Chesed, a more pure experience of the true "Self" than Yesod can offer the awareness of Malkuth. Here, in Binah, the self too is forfeit. But this is just half the story.

From above, it is possible to see Binah as the truly bounteous sphere that it is. Pure divine energy cascades out of Kether, and gains a sense of purpose in Chokmah. It then pours into the oceans of Binah, where it is allotted into portions and passed into the endless bounty of Chesed. From the viewpoint of the top of the Tree, Binah is the Maiden, the bright, fertile mother that gives birth to all.

Even for the human awareness, Binah is a lot less forbidding than it appears. The absence of differentiation is not a loss, it is a gain. To be part of Binah is to be united with infinite understanding and awareness. Within its energies, all are intermixed and mingled, seamless for all intents and purposes, but each part of the whole remembers itself and retains intangible connections. To swim within Binah is to make contact with all forms of consciousness, from those far simpler than humanity's to those far more complex. There is no judgement or analysis, no differentiation, just the perfect understanding of commonality and divine love.

The blackness of Binah is not an absence of light or a signifier of evil – or even of harsh necessity. It is the absorption of all the light that falls upon it: total acceptance and reception. Not all darkness is a cloak for malice. The ego, in particular, finds Binah to be a frightening prospect. The idea that the self does not matter is

profoundly threatening to its most persistent voice. Binah, however, is the loss of the last illusions, the place where we are forced to rediscover our own heritage as a mote of pure love, surrounded on all sides by other motes of pure love, part of God's own limitless light. How could that be anything other than positive? We are all one in God's love, part of his great Sundering so that he may know himself, and experience joy in the interplay of life. Binah simply asks us to remember that we once understood that.

Meditational imagery for Binah usually focuses on the dual aspect of the sphere. The Sephira is seen as an infinitely vast ocean of jet-black water. The gateway for the lower Tree is a small island of black rock where paths arrive, no more than twenty yards across. At its centre,

a small triangular plinth of marble holds three white pillars. The plinth itself has three layers, black at its base, grey in the centre and white at the top. In the middle of the plinth, a small stand holds a jet-black globe. A wall of grey stone runs around the island. By concentrating on it, we can make it lower a little into the sea – not much, but enough to be able to jump over it and into the waters of infinite consciousness and love. Infinity has no borders – the sea can never be crossed by any attempt to swim it or travel through it. However, it *can* be traversed – by merging with it, stretching and expanding the sense of self until at one with the whole infinite ocean. Then awareness of the second gate is possible, where the paths of the higher Tree connect. The traveller, as the embodiment of the sea itself, can

ABOVE: **Associated with water, feminine energies, protection and the power to break love spells, lilies are linked to Binah.**

LEFT: **The fusion of water with spirit, the pearl is the token of divine female energy and all that is creative and nurturing.**

step up onto the small island of the second gate. This island too has a plinth, but its colours are reversed, with a black top layer and pillars, and a white globe and bottom layer.

Binah is associated with black, oceans, the right-hand side of the brain, myrrh, lilies, birch trees, pearl, chalices, whales, sirens, the virtue of silence, sacred glades, empowered employees and moments of inspiration.

Chokmah, Wisdom

Illuminating Intelligence:
"God said: 'Let there be light'"

ה כ מ ת

H   M   K   Ch

ABOVE: Orchids are the flower of heart-centred joy and positivity. They dissolve dark expectations and fears and let in light and love.

RIGHT: A traditional symbol of wisdom and awareness, owls are said to be the wisest of all the birds.

The second sphere, Chokmah (pronounced hokk-MAR) is translated as "Wisdom" or, sometimes, intelligence, and it is occasionally referred to as the holy father, or as the word of God. Planetary associations for the Sephiroth were developed long before the outer planets of the solar system were known about, but modern Kabbalists have suggested that Chokmah can be associated with Neptune. Chokmah is the sphere of divine purpose, and sits at the head of the pillar of mercy.

There have to be two points for a line to exist. There has to be another before the idea of "self" has any meaning. There has to be a mirror before it is possible to view oneself. Chokmah is the first extraction of "other" from the divine. It is the point that gives meaning to distance, the away that the spark of consciousness can move to in order to look back and see the source. By thus gaining some perspective, the divine light can gain the first experiences of itself and therefore gain some knowledge of its own nature. This enlightenment is wisdom.

Filled with the joy of its enlightenment, the divine principle bursts out of Chokmah and radiates in all directions. This outpouring is the origin of all that is. The universe exists – and continues to exist – only because of Chokmah's eternal ecstatic meditation and the life energy that results from it. This is the meaning of the philosophical statement that

we are "held in the mind of God." L'chaiam, the Hebrew toast, comes from the same root as Chokmah does, and means "life." All that is stems from Chokmah and its outpouring of love and life.

At this point in the tree, Chokmah's energy is infinite, eternal and totally undirected. It is the animating principle, unchannelled. It exists in everything – physical matter, thoughts, shapes and principles, movements – without any let or hindrance. It is the very embodiment of energy and action, without any direction or purpose: a fire that does not use up any fuel.

There is no real differentiation in Chokmah, no awareness or perception, no point to be made or lesson to be learnt – just the enlightened awareness of what it means to be part of God. This is not a sphere that the consciousness of humanity can readily approach, at least not until the mind has truly learned the lessons of Binah, and become one with all. This sphere is simply energy – ecstatic, pure, loving divine energy.

Chokmah is usually envisioned as a vast, beautiful white flame, burning eternally. It damages nothing, needs no fuel, and is perfectly safe to gaze upon or touch. To understand it is to become the flame, but few human minds have achieved this.

Chokmah is associated with grey, flame, the left-hand side of the brain, frankincense, orchids, beech trees, the gemstone turquoise, the word, owls, lemurs, the virtue of purpose, sacred trees, corporate vision and moments of reflection.

Kether, Crown

Admirable Intelligence: "In the beginning, God created the heavens and the earth"

ר ת כ

R   Th   K

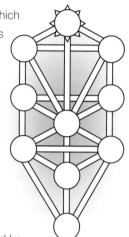

The first sphere of all, Kether (pronounced KEH-terr) is the Crown, the source of the divine, the closest that anything in our universe can get to experiencing God. It has lately been associated with Pluto, and is coloured white. All the light of existence stems from its holy radiance. It is the point at which the divine becomes conscious – the great "I AM." It is associated with white, crowns, the consciousness, almond scent, lotuses, almond trees, diamond, the hermit's lamp, swans, dryads, the virtue of unity, integrity in business, and the life of nature.

Kether is.

To say anything else would be redundant. When you fully understand and experience all the implications of that statement, your journey through the orchard will be complete.

LEFT: Swans were thought of as the king of birds. Embodiments of the divine, they carried messages and power between worlds.

BELOW: The purity, radiance and eternity of diamond make it the most sought after of all gemstones.

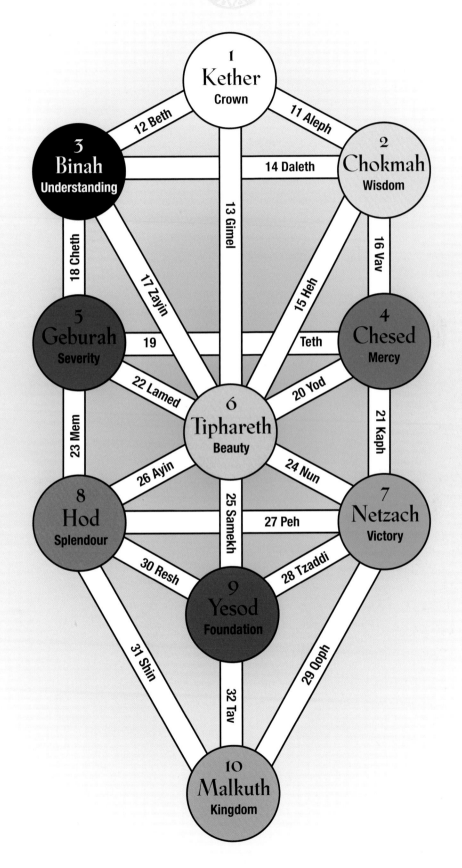

The Nativoth, Paths of the Tree

The 22 paths of the Tree are named for and associated with the 22 letters of the Hebrew alphabet. They represent refinements and subtle, blended aspects of the spheres that they link. Their energies are less primal than the Sephiroth – no less important, but in some senses they are contained within the spheres that they link. As such, they are generally studied less intensively than the Sephiroth. We do not have the room to go into extended information on the Nativoth in this work, but we will look at each one in brief, enabling serious students to begin their own explorations.

Path 32, *Tav* (Cross, 400)

ת

Malkuth to Yesod

"God saw every thing that He had made and beheld that it was very good"

The first half-dozen paths are the seat of the mortal personality, and Tav in particular is the path of the conscious mind. Caught between the objective reality of Malkuth and the imagination and unconscious of Yesod, this is the home of our personality's sense of self. It is the interface between imagination and reality, the gate to the underworld and, as the path by which instinct becomes elaborated, it is also the beginning of art and law. To travel deliberately along Tav is to descend from the bright countryside of reality into the midnight forests of illusion, and the path is a frightening one to those who do not know how powerless illusory beasts actually are.

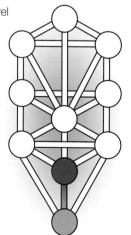

Path 31, *Shin* (Tooth, 300)

ש

Malkuth to Hod

"God made the beast of the earth after its kind"

Shin is the path of logical thought, the home of the personality when it is consciously assessing a situation or object. The experience of Malkuth is carried up to Hod for analysis – and the rationalizations of Hod are taken down to Malkuth for actualization. It is a fire in which ego and instinct are dissolved, so that pure analysis can take place. It is also a place of defence, where the safety of the self is judged. Hod understands the difference between necessity, harm and danger, and banishes confusion with the word "No." It is Shin that forbids you to touch the flame a second time. To walk the path of Shin is to be stripped of gross imperfections and dangers in the deserts of necessity.

Path 30, *Resh* (Head, 200)

ר

Yesod to Hod

"God saw that the beasts of the earth were good"

Resh is the path of implicit knowledge and understanding. When you read your native language, you do not have to

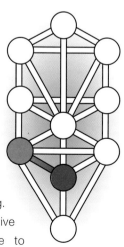

consciously decipher each word. When you catch a ball, you do not work out differential equations describing its ballistic qualities. Resh is the path of that knowledge which has been learnt, absorbed and assimilated. Yesod supplies memories, visions and meanings, which are tested along Resh for relevance, utility and clarity. Those which have enough substance not to evaporate in the glaring sun will reach Hod for formulation. Patterns of action are passed back along Resh for loading into the unconscious and then reality. To walk along Resh's rocky pathway is to have your dreams, fancies, fears and whimsies tested harshly in the scorching light of midday – for usefulness and truth.

Path 29, Qoph (Back of head, 100)

ק

Malkuth to Netzach
"God said I have given you all"

Qoph is the path of expressed emotion. It is the seat of the personality during those times when we are being driven by our feelings. The energy of Netzach is filtered into different strands of emotion along this path – the various harmonic frequencies resonate at different points, alternating with spots of maximum dissonance. At each nexus, like calls to like. Qoph thrums and twists with the power of the energies it channels. It is beautiful and beguiling to walk this path, a series of wondrous glades that embody your entire emotional spectrum, but to complete it you must pass beyond them all, carrying just the fundamental energy of divine love.

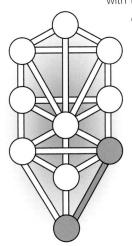

Path 28, Tzaddi (Fish-hook, 90)

צ

Yesod to Netzach
"God blessed them, male and female"

Tzaddi is the path of intuition. The harmony of the body, mind and soul depends upon this conduit between the emotive force in Netzach and the deep foundation wells of Yesod. Psychic forces are expressed here, where the unconscious mind taps into greater awareness of the universal energy. This is the path by which humans contact the gods and goddesses of legend, the source of psychic information, and the personal connection to the will of the universe. Walking the path of Tzaddi involves navigating the labyrinths of the deeper mind – rationality and stubborn determination will not help. To find the way is to move in tune with the universe's purpose.

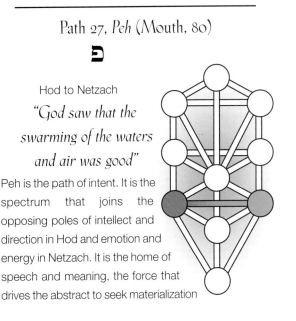

Path 27, Peh (Mouth, 80)

פ

Hod to Netzach
"God saw that the swarming of the waters and air was good"

Peh is the path of intent. It is the spectrum that joins the opposing poles of intellect and direction in Hod and emotion and energy in Netzach. It is the home of speech and meaning, the force that drives the abstract to seek materialization

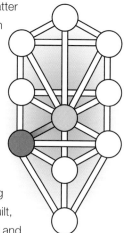

and solidification through the spoken word. As such, it is also thought of as the seat of magic – the art of causing change through intention. Walking the path of Peh requires that the rational mind let go of its certainty and inflexibility; some old ideas must be allowed to fall before new ones have space to evolve. The way is full of hidden mis-steps and stumbling blocks, for conviction produces convicts, but becomes much smoother when prideful certainty is discarded.

Path 26, Ayin (Eye, 70)

ע

Hod to Tiphareth
"Male and female God created them"

If the bottom six paths of the Tree are the home of the personality, then the middle eight paths are associated with the higher Self, the soul that seeks incarnation into the body. The path of Ayin is that of higher conscious-ness. The light of Tiphareth shines along it, illuminating

Hod's perception of gross matter with awareness of the divine in everything. This is the path of the shaman, who works with the spirits of natural objects and locations to bring healing and fertility, and to unearth hidden knowledge. Walking the path of Ayin involves letting go of those things that hinder your growth – stepping free of restrictions such as guilt, remembered pain, bad advice and old rules. It is only possible to scale the cliffs of Ayin once all of these heavy weights have been cast off.

BELOW: **The shaman seeks to work with the divine spark of each object, with the spirit of each stream and rock and tree.**

een Schaman ofte Duyvel-priester.
in 't Tungoesen land

Path 25, Samekh (Support, 60)

ס

Yesod to Tiphareth

"God created man in His own image"

Samekh is the path of temperance. It is the light of spiritual understanding that underlies the unconscious, the empty yearning that all people feel for meaning and purpose in life. It also represents our personal inspiration and our deepest wells of courage, generosity and willpower. Samekh sorts through the 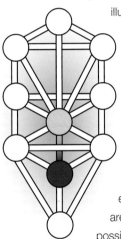 illusions and fantasies of Yesod, exposing them to the light of Tiphareth's wisdom and understanding, so that only the truth may pass upward. To travel the path of Samekh is to face the confusion of false divisions and unnecessary compartments. One has to look beyond the dark, frightening trees and accept that they are all part of the forest before it is possible to rise above the canopy and into the daylight. Bigotry cannot pass this path.

Path 24, Nun (Fish, 50)

נ

Netzach to Tiphareth

"God blessed the sea-monsters, creepers, and fowl"

Nun is the path of transformation. The Self yearns for completion and perfection, and needs the energy and desire of Netzach to drive the personality, so that it can be improved. This path is the channel by which the beauty and divine love of Tiphareth gains the force to power Netzach's engines. The pure golden light is split and channelled down this path, so that it arrives at

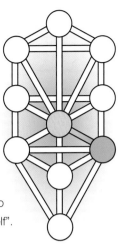

Netzach like a rainbow. To travel back along the path of Nun is to reunite the disparate strands of emotion and energy inside yourself, and recognize all feeling as different emissions of the divine love. Along this route, the personality's wants and drives will be pared away, so that the "self" can see the "Self".

ABOVE: **The pure energy of the soul is split along the path of Nun into the rainbow light that contains all feeling.**

Path 23, Mem (Water, 40)

מ

Hod to Geburah

"God made the two great lights"

Mem is the path of self-sacrifice. Geburah's iron discipline and ruthless love clash somewhat with
Hod's urge to classify and communicate, but both spheres understand the underlying need for
rationality. This path is like a laser
– focused justice turned to the
purpose of purification. It is utterly
single-minded, devoid of all senti-
mentality and pity. Passing the
city of brass can only be achieved
by sacrifice of the lower urges. Only
the resolute pursuit of higher truths
can provide the required dedication.

Path 22, Lamed (Ox-goad, 30)

ל

Tiphareth to Geburah

*"God created the sea-monsters,
creatures that creep, and fowl"*

Lamed is the path of discipline.
Divine energy brings us the
lessons that we require, so that
we can learn the things that we
need. It is not always easy or
pleasant, but this path requires
us to accept that our duty to
God is to try to undo the
Sundering, and to seek return
through perfection. Sometimes
that means just getting down to
business. The old, haphazard forms

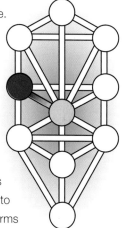

of growth have become outmoded. The Self has to be
assessed, old patterns examined, new improvements
suggested. Purposes and methods must be examined
and implemented. To walk the path of Lamed is to cross
the burning plain, one painful step at a time, ignoring
temptations and shortcuts. There is no other way.

Path 21, Kaph (Palm, 20)

כ

Netzach to Chesed

*"God saw that that the lights in the
firmament were good"*

Kaph is the path of progress. The higher and the lower
are united here in common desire for the riches of divinity.
This is the place of natural progression,
where the limitless bounty of God's
love is passed on in its allotted time
and manner according to the
needs of the lower Tree. The
seasons turn here, the stars wheel
overhead, and all things have their
proper place in the cycle. Walking
the pleasant landscapes of Kaph
requires only the unity of higher and
lower purpose, and the patience to
know when it is time to advance, and time
to stand still. All obstacles on this path will
remove themselves naturally, if the desire of
the lower self is in accord with that of the higher Self.

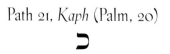

Path 20, Yod (Hand, 10)

י

Tiphareth to Chesed

*"God set the two lights in the firmament
of the heaven"*

Yod is the path of acceptance. Tiphareth is a place of
beauty and splendour, but God's love is far greater and

more beautiful. However, it requires an open mind to accept assistance when one does not know that it is necessary. This path appears odd, even diversionary, but appearances are a deceit, and it leads to great storehouses of love and wisdom. To travel Yod is to turn away from the happy crowd of your fellows and pick a solitary path up into the hills. The only way to complete it is to put aside all thoughts of pride or achievement and open-mindedly accept help and advice that you don't think you need.

Path 19, *Teth* (Serpent, 9)

מ

Geburah to Chesed
"God called the dry land 'Earth'"

Teth is the path of restraint. It is the spectrum that joins the pole of necessity and severity in Geburah with the pole of mercy and plenty in Chesed. It is the home of the dragon force that powers the soul, the energy of the spark of life itself. It is also thought to be the home of the angelic beings, executors of God's will and love. Teth is the wisdom that knows when to stop applying force. To travel the quicksands of Teth involves accepting and facing your deepest fears, and in doing so learning how to control your basic instincts and behaviours.

Path 18, *Cheth* (Fence, 8)

ח

Geburah to Binah
"God called the firmament 'Heaven'"

The top eight paths of the Tree are associated with the pure emanation of divinity in various aspects. They are the roads that can lead the soul back to unity with God. Cheth is the path of Merkabah. It is the deep, pre-conscious structuring of reality, the forms created by God which give rise to the world. Divine purpose, God's ineffable plan, resides within this path. To travel along the path of Cheth, one must pass through the 50 gates of understanding. In each of the lower seven spheres – Chesed, Geburah, Tiphareth, Netzach, Hod, Yesod and Malkuth – the traveller has to pass seven tests of vice by possessing the right thoughts and conduct. When each of the 49 tests has been passed, the 50th gate opens, and passage into Binah becomes possible.

Path 17, *Zayin* (Sword, 7)

ז

Tiphareth to Binah
"God called the light 'Day', and darkness 'Night'"

Zayin is the path of unity. Binah understands that all are one, and seeks to show the soul in Tiphareth. This path is the source of creativity, as the packaged but undefined energies from Binah are showered onto the soul, which can turn them to whatever purpose it sees fit. To progress up Zayin is to recognize that the apparent duality of all things is false, and that in fact all is unity. The self and the Self; the Self and the divine; the animus and anima; the individual and the other – all divisions are dissolved in the purity of God's divine love, and all imbalances righted.

Path 16, Vav (Nail, 6)

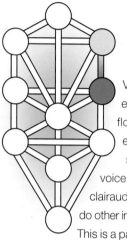

Chesed to Chokmah

"God divided the light from the darkness"

Vav is the path of revelation. The excitement and glory of the divine floods into Chesed, which expresses it in the infinite variety so loved by the Sephira. The voice of God and other inspired clairaudience comes from this path, as do other initiations, secrets and revelations. This is a path of true wisdom, an irrational, excited place where the unexpected can lift the mind toward enlightenment. To travel the path of Vav, you must first silence the inner rambling of the mind and soul. Only then will you be able to hear the true voice of divine wisdom that will guide you up the path.

RIGHT: **The formation of the soul in alchemical thought was strongly influenced by Kabbalistic teachings.**

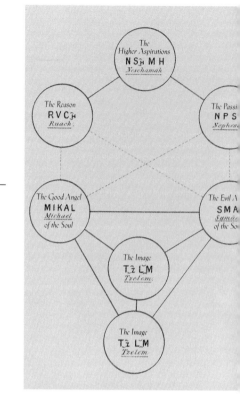

Path 15, Heh (Window, 5)

Tiphareth to Chokmah

"God saw that the earth bringing forth grass was good"

Heh is the path of the Otz Chiim itself. It connects the pure excited divine energy of Chokmah with the beauty and peace of the soul, and as such represents God breathing life into the universe via the Tree entire. It is a fractal path of divine wisdom and life-force that gives birth to the structure of the Tree. Along this path, energy's relationship to the Self finds definition and examination – the ordering and stabilization of

joyful anarchy. Walking this path is an act of faith in the divine and the pointlessness of "fate." Without it, there can be no peace in the face of laughing chaos, and no progress toward Chokmah's pure excitement.

Path 14, Daleth (Door, 4)

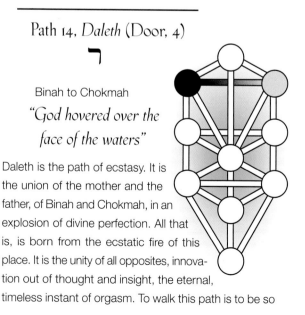

Binah to Chokmah

"God hovered over the face of the waters"

Daleth is the path of ecstasy. It is the union of the mother and the father, of Binah and Chokmah, in an explosion of divine perfection. All that is, is born from the ecstatic fire of this place. It is the unity of all opposites, innovation out of thought and insight, the eternal, timeless instant of orgasm. To walk this path is to be so overwhelmed by the sheer joy of the divine that even the awareness that all is one is stripped away.

Path 13, Gimel (Camel, 3)

ג

Tiphareth to Kether

"God saw that the separation of land and waters was good"

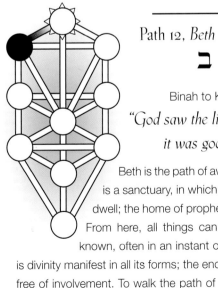

Gimel is the path of trial. Rising from Tiphareth directly to Kether, it is the main route across the abyss for those who do not want to swim the eternal oceans of Binah. It is the longest of all the paths of the Tree, and it is uphill all the way. It is the link between head and heart, between the immortal soul and the word of God itself. Gimel is the channel down which the divine spark of life flows into the self, our ultimate connection back to the source. To tackle Gimel, one must be prepared for a long, isolated effort that frequently feels fraught with futility. Any baggage or imperfection will weigh you down so heavily that the journey becomes impossible, yet all you need to do to complete it is to innocently accept the unity of all mind.

Path 12, Beth (House, 2)

ב

Binah to Kether

"God saw the light, that it was good"

Beth is the path of awareness. This is a sanctuary, in which the divine can dwell; the home of prophecy and vision. From here, all things can be seen and known, often in an instant of gestalt. Beth is divinity manifest in all its forms; the end of all actions, free of involvement. To walk the path of Beth is to see all, but to be touched by nothing.

Path 11, Aleph (Ox, 1)

א

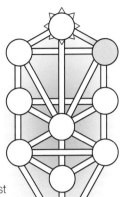

Chokmah to Kether

"God made the Firmament and divided the waters"

Aleph is the path of faith. It is the first cause, the route by which the divine's awareness first learnt to perceive, the moment of the birth of the universe, when the big bang first started to spew out galaxies. To walk this path is to express total trust in the divine, accepting that it is unknowable; to have such a total awareness of the universal potential that there is no sense left of self. Aleph says "I AM," and says it so loudly and precisely that even "I" and "AM" lose their meaning.

BELOW: Aleph, as the foundation of the Hebrew alphabet, is far more than just a letter, as this esoteric rendering of its secrets indicates.

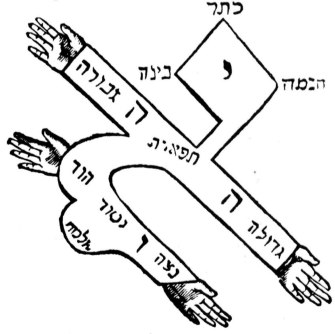

Deeper Mysteries

The structure of the Tree of Life is a mystical journey in its own right. A profoundly versatile map of symbolism and linkage, it reflects not only the aspects we have examined so far – God's creation of the universe, and humanity's way of purification and enlightenment – but also all other structures. With a little consideration, the Tree can be fitted to any complete system, from physical health to the Catholic Church or, as we will see in the next chapter, to the tarot. The art of interpreting the Tree in the light of other systems is known as correspondence, and we will examine that shortly.

First, it is important to note that profound as the Tree of Life is, there are many deeper mysteries that its structure implies or reveals. Each of them has the potential to be as significant as the Tree itself. We do not have room here to go into detailed discussion of their implications, but no examination of the Tree would be complete without at least introducing them.

The Abyss of *Abada*

One of the most notorious features of the Tree of Life is Abada, the infinite abyss. The three Sephiroth at the head of the Tree, Kether, Chokmah and Binah, are known as the supernal triad. Because the notion of duality does not come into being until God's energy is embodied in Chesed, the triad exists in a paradoxical state of unitary consciousness that is utterly alien to the human mind. The only way to truly experience the highest parts of the Tree is to experience that unitary consciousness first-hand. Without it, the mystic will only experience the palest shadows of the triad spheres. Genuine enlightenment involves personal contact with the union of all. This is the ultimate goal of the immortal soul, the great work of truly entering the orchard. It is the same state as the perfect *Turiya* of the Indian yoga masters and the *Nirvana* of the Buddhist monks, and it is every bit as difficult to truly achieve.

LEFT: **The Tree of Life has always been a very popular subject for esoteric and mystic illustration. Here, Malkuth is shown coloured for its four elemental quarters.**

In the Tree of Life, this altering of consciousness is referred to as Abada, the abyss. The supernal triad is separated from the rest of the Tree by *Paroket*, a double row of veiling curtains. The abyss is between the veils, but only those with knowledge of it can even experience it. To everyone else, Paroket is simply a curtain, leading nowhere and hiding nothing.

A small amount of knowledge can be extremely dangerous here. This is the test that Rabbi Akiva put his famous colleagues through – only he could cross, and the other three died, went mad and became murderously heretical. The risk lies in trying to carry psychological baggage into the experience of unity with God. The aim of the lower paths and spheres is to purify the mystic so that he or she is genuinely free of illusions, fears, desires and false impressions. The ego has to be entirely conquered. During the process of unification, all mental barriers are broken down, because all is one. Any hidden aspects inside the mind will be brought forward, magnified until they are the same size as the entire personality, and unified with the rest of the consciousness. There is no re-compartmentalization afterwards. If the mind carries anything other than pure divine love into the abyss, the best possible outcome is unconquerable obsession.

From the point of view of the failed mystic, God has been experienced, and revealed as the psychological baggage that was carried into unity. All sorts of strange cults and madness can result. For example, carrying a lingering hint of the fear of death into the abyss will convince the mind that God is death and terror, and that all existence is decay and horror. The result of that sort of obsession tends to be persistent catatonia. Pride leads to self-identification as the Messiah or even as God; even too much kindness can result in pathological martyrdom.

Crossing the abyss is not to be taken lightly. Fortunately, attaining a genuine state of unitary consciousness is extremely difficult, particularly for a mind that is still shackled with daily concerns. Meditational exercises that simulate the voyage over the abyss are entirely safe – there has to be genuine intent for the mind to approach that sort of union. The rewards are great, however. The awareness itself is ecstasy, the closest that we can get to heaven on earth. For the mystic who successfully achieves enlightenment, all forces are balanced, and the divine light shines directly into Tiphareth, which in turn spreads genuine illumination to all the spheres. This is the state that the Baal Shem were supposed to have access to, the legendary miracle workers who had mastery of the Word.

Customarily, the two main paths across the abyss are the Sephira of Binah and the Nativa of Gimel. The more direct route is Gimel, with the mystic seeking to rise in a straight line from Malkuth, through Yesod, to Tiphareth, and from there to Kether. This is a very intense path, and requires a great deal of peace and quiet from the rest of the world. If you are able to retreat to a monastery or cave – ideally with a teacher – and dedicate yourself to self-purification of body, mind and soul, then Gimel is a good choice.

The slower route involves working with the Tree sequentially, from the bottom upward. This is a process of gradual refinement, attempting to master each Sephira and the Nativoth it touches before moving on to the next. It takes far longer, but does not require the intensive study or withdrawal that the other route does. In this manner, by the time that mystics have worked their way up to the tiny protrusion of Binah that extends below the abyss, they are sufficiently purified to be able to engage the dark oceans in reasonable safety. In particular, the Nativoth of Cheth and Zayin (18 and 17, leading to Binah from Geburah and Tiphareth respectively) are very close to crossing the abyss itself, and if they have been thoroughly mastered, Binah should present no problems.

Da'ath, the false Sephira

Da'ath is knowledge without understanding, learning without illumination. It represents being stopped at the abyss, the limits of the dualist mind that cannot see to Binah or above. The serpent of the flesh can coil its way up the Tree, but it cannot pass to the heights of divinity. Qabalists, in particular, tend to place Da'ath as a "hidden" Sephira on the Path of Gimel between Tiphareth and Kether, below the level of Binah and Chokmah. Despite their good intentions, Da'ath is not a Sephira of any sort, and has no place on the Tree; it is just a concept.

In traditional Hebraic thought, Da'ath is highly negative. It is the proof that denies faith, the false godhead of information for its own sake. If it resides anywhere, then it is inside the abyss itself, a symbol of the danger of trying to cross with an unpurified mind.

Knowledge *per se* is a vital component of a successful, happy life. Without knowledge, the mystic cannot even perceive Abada, let alone approach it. The danger represented by Da'ath is that of mistaking the importance of knowledge compared to insight, wisdom and the spark of the divine.

Perhaps one of the reasons that Da'ath is sometimes mistaken for a Sephira is that knowledge, like the physical universe, is infinite and, of itself, empty. Just consider the irrational number Pi, for example. On its own, it is infinitely large, and yet it consists of nothing more than arrangements of the digits 0 through 9. Da'ath is infinities within infinities within infinities, a glittering maze of elegance and beauty, utterly devoid of meaning. One could spend a lifetime memorizing Pi to a billion digits, and still possess no wisdom or understanding whatsoever. Da'ath is a well-gilded trap.

The Veils of Existence

Kether is the point from which everything springs, the pinprick origin of the Big Bang. It is the spot which first gained awareness in its own right, through which God's pure love and will pour. But it is not God himself, any more than Malkuth is literally the physical world. Kabbalists say that the true face of God is hidden behind three veils, each infinite and impenetrable. The veils soften the force of God's likeness so that his majesty and perfection do not sweep aside all divisions within the Tree and bring about the end of the universe. They are, by their very definition, beyond our understanding and awareness. There is no path to them, no abyss to cross them, no way to project on forwards. They are a symbol of our limited ability to understand God.

The first veil is portrayed as a solid arc, like that of a distant horizon. It is called *Ain Soph Aur*, or "Limitless Light." Behind that, the second veil is identically shaped, but is represented by a line of long dashes. It is called *Ain Soph*, or "Limitless Infinity". Finally, the third veil runs just behind the other two, but is depicted as a line of short dashes. It is called simply *Ain*, or "Limitless Void."

The three veils are really just one, indivisible and inseparable, and splitting them notionally only really makes sense in terms of the human need to classify and understand. In many senses, it can be argued that Kether, Chokmah and Binah are really a single influence, because they all exist within the state of undifferentiated unity. As such, it may be that the veils are divided to draw

LEFT: **The mystic path is commonly thought to be linked with retreat, meditation and various ascetic forms of self-improvement.**

RIGHT: **The macrocosm reflects the microcosm in this seventeenth-century Alchemical/Kabbalistic crossover image by Von Rosenroth.**

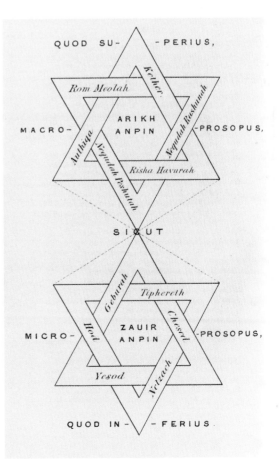

ABOVE: **The veils of existence mark the very outside limits of the possibilities for human understanding and perception.**

wisdom to attain understanding of the godhead in Kether. However, the left-hand pillar of Hod, Geburah and Binah, the Pillar of Severity, is also considered a route to enlightenment, as is the right-hand Pillar of Mercy, comprising Netzach, Chesed and Chokmah.

Progressing toward enlightenment via the Pillar of Severity involves the relentless application of will in scouring and perfecting the self. Conversely, climbing the Pillar of Mercy is an act of total surrender, of giving up all that the self holds until nothing remains. Neither path is simple to pursue. Traditionally, the left-hand path has been associated with black magic, and acts of cruelty and even evil, but this is a misunderstanding. It demands rigorous discipline, certainly to the exclusion of social niceties, but malice has no place on the Tree, and would set the initiate back several steps. Similarly, the right-hand path is by its nature highly generous and selflessly benevolent, and is often thought of as "good," but that too is something of a misperception. Both pillars lead to the same place as the middle pillar – the understanding that all is one – but the left-hand approaches it through the idea that everything is inside the self, while the right-hand posits that the self is illusory.

parallels with the supernal triad. In fact, in some depictions of the Tree of Life, the veils are designated by one united sphere, the top half white and the bottom half black, called the "Horizon of Eternity." To speculate on the veils is to indulge in pure philosophy for its own sake, for they are forever outside the understanding of even the most enlightened human mind.

The Three Pillars

Looking at the layout of the Sephiroth, it is immediately clear that they are arranged in three vertical columns. Closer examination of the spheres in each column uncovers a certain kindred nature between the Sephiroth. These are the three pillars of the Tree, and they are generally taken to represent polarities along a moral spectrum.

As we discussed a short while ago, the middle pillar, known as the Pillar of Balance, represents a direct, meditational route to enlightenment. It is a set of way-stations by which the initiate may seek purification. Malkuth, Yesod and Tiphareth are all aspects of the self – lower, unconscious and higher respectively – and by refining them, achieving balance, the initiate seeks the

The Qliphoth

The Tree of Life is said to have a negative reflection. Kabbalistic thought has long suggested that as all actions in the world are informed by shards of God, and many actions are evil or lead to evil, then evil must be one of God's tools. In this model of the celestial scheme, Satan did not rebel so much as volunteer to take on a dirty job. The Tree of Life is the perfect model of the universe, but what model could be perfect if it did not mirror the great imperfections of reality? This led to the realization that the Tree must have a dark side.

Each sphere has a negative counterpart, an empty, hollow husk that it shed as part of its progress. These husks, or Qliphoth, embody the dark side of each of the Sephiroth, and are the sources of the dark vices and evils within the world. Where angels and archetypal spirits reside in the Sephiroth, the husks are home to demons and monsters, and to work with them is to open yourself to corruption and disease.

In theory, there are paths through from each Sephira to its Qliphotic equivalent, although these are not usually easy to find. Yesod is particularly prone to linking with its Qlipha, because so much of its content is so dark and confused already. However, the major interface point between the two sides of the Tree is Abada, the abyss. By following the skeins of obsession down into the depths of the abyss, it is possible to come out into the diseased side of the Tree. Some suggest that there are beneficial uses to working with the Qliphoth, but in general it is considered far more sensible to avoid them.

Sometimes it is said that the Tree of Life contains the four worlds. In these instances, Atziluth is represented by Kether and Chokmah, Briah by Binah, Yetzirah by the spheres from Chesed down to Yesod, and Assiah by Malkuth. However, it is just as common to say that each of the four worlds contains its own entire Tree of Life, and that the Malkuth of each gives rise to the Kether of the next.

Sinking down through the worlds, Atziluth is a realm of infinite unity, the perception of the divine. This multiplies itself by another order of infinity to bring about specific but non-sequential meaning in Briah – an infinite

The Four Worlds

It is generally thought that the universe did not form all in one instance. Kabbalistic thought says that there are four different worlds – planes of existence – and that the universe was brought into existence across them sequentially rather than simultaneously. The first world is *Atziluth*, the divine world of Emanation, attributed to fire, where all is unitary. The second world is *Briah*, the creative world of Thrones, attributed to water, a realm of non-sequential meaning. The third world is *Yetzirah*, the Formative world, attributed to air, where meaning and symbolism exist. The fourth and final world, *Assiah*, is the Manifest world of sequential reality and spatial meaning, the earth that we ourselves live in.

RIGHT: **The Tree of Life is depicted here set against the Ascended Man, balanced between the pillars of Mercy and Severity.**

variety, but without sequence, order or true division; the ocean in which each drop is one with the whole, but separate. Briah then multiplies itself by another order of infinity to make room for sequence and relationship, Yetzirah. Here one thing leads to another, time, thought, emotion and logic. Yetzirah then finally multiplies itself one last time to make room for the spatial ordering and relationship of our conventional world.

Creation in Atziluth is beyond description; it is the Word of the beginning. By comparison, creation in the Briatic world is that described in the book of Genesis. It is said that the *Sepher Yetzirah* goes on to describe the orderly, sequential creation of the Yetziratic world. The science of the Big Bang is left to describe creation in Assiah.

The Sephiroth of the Tree take form quite differently in each of the worlds. God acts directly in Atziluth, and the Sephiroth take on the mantle of the ten names of God. It is the ten archangels who discharge God's will in Briah, however. The choirs of angels represent the Sephiroth in Yetzirah. Finally, the Sephiroth of the standard Tree are the vehicles of God's will in our realm of Assiah.

The attributions of the four worlds are a great assistance in plotting correspondences between the Tree of Life and four-fold systems. It is also worth noting that in correspondence with seven-fold systems, such as the Seven Chakras or the Seven Planes of Being, Malkuth and Yesod are normally thought of as corresponding to the lowest item, and the supernal triad of Binah, Chokmah and Kether are associated together with the highest. The other Sephiroth fall individually into place between them.

Gematria

The art of Gematria is a kind of mystically-inspired word game. It is all about finding connections and linkages between things, and investigating deeper meanings of words and phrases that seem obscure. The basic process itself is simple enough. Each letter of the Hebrew alphabet has a numerical value, as listed in the section discussing the Nativoth. The values range from 1 to 400 – in early Hebrew, the letters also doubled as numerical digits. The end result of this is that every word has a value.

Because God created the sacred texts, particularly the Torah, with full understanding of the complexity of his creation, words (or phrases) in sacred texts that possess the same value are assumed to be linked in some way. This equivalence is thought to never be coincidental. As each letter is one of the Nativoth, it is also a different creative force in its own right. Numeric equivalence reveals a connection between the creative potential of the two words, even in non-sacred writing.

To use a fairly famous example, the words DChA (*Achad*, or "Unity") and HBHA (*Ahebah*, or "Love") both total 13. Therefore, they are equivalent; love is unity, and unity is love. Implications can be profound; this particular linkage underlies a lot of the Kabbalah.

A number of factors complicate Gematria. The first is that some letters have two values. *Kaph*, *Mem*, *Nun*, *Peh* and *Tzaddi* all have alternate physical shapes depending on whether they appear at the end of a word or not. These terminator variants are assigned further values in the numeric sequence of 500, 600, 700, 800 and 900 respectively. To complete the sequence, *Aleph* is then said to wrap around to be both the beginning and the end of the alphabet, and to take the value 1,000 as well as the value 1, although it has no second form. In Gematria, all six of these alternate values are used at the discretion of the sage, and the terminator letters are as likely to hold their usual value as their higher value.

Further options are introduced with alternate methods of calculating numeric value associated with the four worlds of creation. The method that we have just outlined is called the *Mispar Hechrachi* ("Absolute Value"), and it is associated with the world of Atziluth. The world of Briah is associated with the system of *Mispar Siduri* ("Ordinal Value"), in which the letters are numbered from 1 to 22 in order, with the five terminators taking the values 23 to 27.

In the system of *Mispar Katan* ("Reduced Value"), associated with the world of Yetzirah, the digits of each letter's value are summed until they have been reduced to just one digit (mathematicians call this "Modulo 9"). Thus Aleph, at 1, remains 1, while Yod (10), becomes 1+0=1, and Qoph (100 or 19) also becomes 1. Note that

the ordinal value of Qoph has to be reduced twice – 1+9 = 10, and then 1+0 = 1.

Finally, the system of *Mispar Katan Mispari* ("Integral Reduced Value") is associated with the world of Assiyah. This version adds the letters of the word up to get a total value, and then sums the digits of the word until each word is valued from 0 to 9. Interestingly, you get exactly the same result whether you work with the Absolute, Ordinal or Reduced values of each letter.

Further complexity arises with the idea of "pregnant" letters – that is, any particular letter in a word can either take its own value, or the value it would have if you spelt it out in full. Many letters have a number of alternate spellings, and each of these has its own value – and therefore its own implications. To give you a very brief example, the letter *Vav* can be properly spelt in Hebrew as VAV, VIV or VV, giving it alternate values of 13, 22 and 12 (and, by reduction, 4 and 3) in addition to its more usual value of 6. If you've noticed that Vav therefore has as many different possible values (3, 4, 6, 12, 13 and 22) as its usual value (6), you're starting to think gematrically.

It should be obvious that Gematria is a very complex art, guided as much by divine inspiration and understanding as mathematical prowess, and many sages have spent entire lifetimes devoted to its subtleties. The different options for calculation are not considered to be mathematical sophistry; for the serious gematrician, they represent different aspects of God's wisdom and glory. Some western thinkers have argued that any alphabet can be used gematrically, but that does seem to be missing the point. A few have even gone so far as to encode gematric meaning into manuscripts of their own creation, forming clues to deeper meanings or elaborate jokes but it is doubtful whether this has extended to modern times.

In addition to Gematria, there are two even more abstruse forms of mathematical analysis that can be applied to text. Very briefly, *Temurah* is a system of permutation, whereby letters can be substituted for other letters according to shared characteristics such as being one of the three mother letters, or possessing the same reduced value. *Notariqon* is a system of hidden abbreviation, and takes two complementary forms. In the first, each of the letters of a word are taken as the initials of the words of a relevant phrase – as in the urban legend that claimed that Adidas, the sport shoe brand name, was short for "All Day I Dream About Sport." In fact, the brand is named after its creator, Adi Dassler. The alternate form of Notariqon is, unsurprisingly, to discover a phrase whose initial letters make up a word and analyze the phrase in light of that word. Notariqon implies complicated energies.

The Art of Correspondence

As the blueprint of creation, the Tree of Life manifests itself in all things, and at all levels of existence. It is the original fractal building block, representing both the act of creating something and the object itself, both the path by which God's love gains consciousness as the human mind and the route by which man can approach God. It is duality and unity, complete and yet all-encompassing, and its influence expands into all things at all times.

Correspondence is the art of mapping the Tree to a particular concept, object, process or setting. Doing so makes it possible to consider parallels between different aspects of life, to look at subtle interrelations that are internal to the concept in question, to evaluate different elements of the mapped thing in relation to each other, to apply many of the lessons learned from the abstract Tree to real life, and, not least, to inter-relate elements of various things to each other. The Tree is a tool of both analysis and manifestation, and it is possible to glean all sorts of fascinating and unpredictable insights from correspondence.

The practical side of Kabbalistic research – the miracles worked by the Baal Shem – is also founded on correspondence. The human body has long been mapped to the Sephiroth and Nativoth, for example. In treating a disease or ailment, the Baal Shem would look at the correspondences between the symptoms and the areas affected to work out which areas of the Tree indicate the imbalances within the patient's body. Healing would then be achieved through prayers and talismans directed to the specific angels, archangels and names of God associated with that part of the tree.

For example, jaundice is associated with the Nativa of Ayin, which joins Hod to Tiphareth. Knowing this, a Baal Shem with a jaundiced patient would seek to work with the lower right back (the area of the body that Ayin corresponds to), perhaps painting ochre-gold talismans there which called on *IHVH Aloah* and *Elohim Tzabaoth*, the names of God in Tiphareth and Hod respectively. He might also have sought to treat the patient with herbs and medicines known to strengthen the heart and the kidneys (again, those parts being associated with Tiphareth and Hod), and to burn nutmeg oil as an aromatic to cleanse the room. On a spiritual level, he may have sought to ascertain whether the patient was labouring under a particular burden of old guilt or pain, or was feeling restricted by badly thought-out rule or advice, for those are the particular challenges that Ayin has to offer.

The western Qabalists in particular have been very keen to build up huge tables of correspondences. Western occultism makes heavy use of a technique called syncretization, by which local mythologies and belief systems absorb a coating of some other, more familiar system. Voodoo is the most famous syncretic cult; its Loa and spirits absorbed a lot of Catholic imagery, particularly related to the various saints. This allowed slaves to worship their own deities while appearing to their masters to have at least partially converted to Christianity.

In other words, syncretization is basically building correspondences between two systems and then hiding one within the other. However, it can be cumbersome, particularly when there are a lot of interrelating systems. The Tree of Life and the art of correspondence therefore appealed greatly to the Qabalists, because it gave them a master-key that they could apply to each system without then having to worry about the details of fitting more abstract elements of disparate systems together.

However, there is a considerable amount of controversy regarding the tables of correspondence that can be obtained today. Orthodox Kabbalists are very wary of the western correspondences, questioning the accuracy and meaning of many of them. Like all such areas, the truth is mutable, and different views may reflect different aspects of God's design. Most practising Kabbalists are

LEFT: This amulet draws on the power of applied Kabbalah to cure a sick person of the disease of jaundice.

encouraged to build up their own correspondences through meditation and insight into the workings of the world; these personal interpretations and linkages are always highly valuable to the individual Kabbalist.

To work out correspondences of your own, the best approach is to start by identifying core aspects of the system you are attempting to analyze, and then think about possible parallels with the Sephiroth. It is usually necessary to go back and forth between the two several times before you start to feel comfortable that your analysis makes a meaningful map. Gematria can give hints, if you know enough Hebrew to work with it effectively. Taking the four worlds and the three pillars into account can also help you during your analysis. You will need to make some abstractions: everything that is contains at least a little of each of the Sephiroth and Nativoth – including each separate Sephira and Nativa,

even – so most early correspondences are close approximations rather than exact identities.

Once you feel comfortable in your interpretation of the Sephiroth, consider the Nativoth in terms of the system you are corresponding the Tree to. They may have obvious parallels in your system, or they might give you startling new insights by making you consider linkages that you had not thought of before. In time, you will build up several correspondences, and can start to analyze parts of a system in terms of parallel parts of other systems. This works for even the most unlikely elements – what does it tell you that Captain Kirk is equivalent to the bodywork of a car, while Mr. Spock is linked to the steering wheel?

In all seriousness, the art of correspondence is the key to truly benefiting from the study of the Kabbalah. It is impossible to overstate its importance.

The Mystical Kabbalah

The teachings and wisdom of the Kabbalah have been an indispensable part of the mystical traditions of the West for centuries. In fact, the two have become so intertwined that it is impossible to imagine what western mysticism would look like without the Kabbalah. Although the reverse is not quite true, it would also be highly unfair to suggest that western mystical thinkers had never been able to make any valuable contributions to Kabbalistic understanding.

Over the course of this chapter, we will look at what it means to think mystically. Afterward, we will examine some of the paths of mystic development, and the ways that they relate to the Kabbalah. Finally, we will consider its effects on two of the most important strands of western mystical thought – alchemy and the tarot.

The Mystical Mindset

Mystics are men and women devoted to exploring the spiritual and divine nature of the world, but there is not much overlap between traditional organized religion and mystic practice. Traditional religion aims to explain the trials and tribulations of life, to give meaning and purpose to the pain and hardship of existence. Organized religion sets out to offer a set of structures and purposes that can help people make sense of the world around them. Mystics, on the other hand, have little interest in the daily grind. Historically, the vast majority of prominent mystics whose revelations have left legacies or brought them acclaim have spent an extended period of time secluded away from humanity. Many live as hermits for years before returning to share their discoveries. Their teachings are

often highly abstract, because their experiences are so profound and distant from everyday life. Some mystics have little interest left in the world's less abstract side, paying little attention to ephemera such as fashion or physical beauty. The love and joy radiating from any enlightened person is unmistakable and awe-inspiring, teaching by example that it is possible to know God more directly than any priest's congregation member ever can. Fortunately, the Kabbalah is well suited to providing a gentler path to mystical enlightenment that does not have to involve any loss of contact with the world or its social niceties.

RIGHT: **The shaman, who operates on the level of the spiritual forces of reality, embodies the animist style of understanding the world.**

BELOW LEFT: **Christian mystic and thinker Saint Jerome spent five years doing penitence in the desert before producing a prodigious body of works.**

So, from the point of view of the organized religions, mystics are slightly embarrassing, and usually bad for business. They look odd, they frequently sound a little unhinged, they have a closer connection to the divine than the priests do, and they have a habit of encouraging other people to search for the same understanding within themselves as well. It is small wonder that many of them have been persecuted and vilified over the centuries.

The mystic understands that there are forces behind material reality that are structured in a different manner, and is resolved to gain a deeper understanding of them. There are several broad categories of mystical thought and practice. Animists believe that each object and phenomenon has its own, unique, sentient spirit, invisible to most but still part of the natural world. Shamans believe that there is a separate spirit world inhabited usually by archetypal spirits (such as Bear, who represents all bears) and the souls of the dead. Finally, Deist mystics believe in a divine force underlying the world. Deists divide into three separate strands of intention. Theosophists (and Gnostics) seek to gain deeper knowledge and understanding of the divine, in order to live better lives and to make sense of the world. Theurgists (and magicians)

Тунгуской Шаманъ при рѣкѣ Аргунъ сзади.
Ein Tungusischer Schamann am Argun Fluß rückwarts
Devin toungouse auprès de l'Argoun par derrière.

seek to control and channel the divine energies, in order to affect the world in their favour. Ecstatic mystics –normally thought of as just "mystics" – seek to experience direct contact with the force, and the deep sense of joy that it brings. The Kabbalah is a powerful system for all Deist mystics, because it can be used to understand God's design, the way that the universe works *and* the personal self. That is why it has become so widely accepted by so many different groups, from serious Talmudic scholars to English ritual magicians.

The Mystical Path

Mystic work requires, above all, dedication. All self-improvement and personal change is difficult – anyone who says differently is selling something, probably a stop-smoking patch or a "delicious and filling" meal-substitute shake. At least a diet produces a tangible sense of progress. The mystical path is long, and often seems pointless. Without dedication – and a modicum of faith – there is very little chance of seeing it through. Another vital requirement is that the mystic should be prepared to change. The path to enlightenment is one of refinement, and that's true of every mystical tradition, not just the Kabbalah. A would-be mystic must be prepared to face the darker side of the personality and let go of some of its consolations.

Moving past the beginning stages of mystical development is not especially hard, despite what many would-be teachers like to claim. Like everything else in life, it takes repeated practice and the will to improve. This is where dedication pays off. No matter how hard the way looks, or how pointless a particular exercise seems, or how difficult or painful it is to deal with some of the blacker parts of the personality, the mystic has to keep on the path. The first rewards come quickly, manifesting as an increasing sense of personal peace and joy, and a deeper feeling of connection to the world and to humankind. Patience is one of the most important qualities here, along with a sense of perspective to help make sure that pride, greed and excessive compassion do not lead the seeker astray.

Finally, the enlightened mystic experiences the unity of all life and its foundation in the divine light of love – again, something that remains true across all mystic traditions. This typically leads to a deep personal wellspring of bliss and universal love. The mind usually gains profound understanding of the world and the nature of divinity, although this may be difficult to express in non-artistic terms. Traditionally, attaining enlightenment is associated with the ability to heal the sick through energy transfer, as well as other miraculous/psychic abilities, such as telepathy, clairvoyance and astral projection.

While the road to mystical consciousness is undoubtedly long, and frequently difficult, there is no person on the face of the planet who is prohibited from attaining it successfully. All that you require is the genuine desire to experience the bliss of unity, and the determination to keep at it until you reach your goal. This is one of the Kabbalah's strongest and most important teachings – everybody can find their way back to unity with God, and in fact everybody *should*. The prophesied Messiah will not be able to visit Earth and usher in the new golden age until all the sundered shards have made the journey back up the Tree to renew their connection with God. The Kabbalah teaches us that it is everyone's destiny to make the journey up the Tree.

Entering the Orchard

Mystical enlightenment is frequently misunderstood. This is not surprising, since it is an experience far outside the realms of language, so it is very difficult to talk about effectively. The basic principle, however, is that you must lower the barriers that separate you from the divine essence within you, and make a direct, personal connection to the spark of God that animates your soul. The result is a deep, powerful sense of bliss and a profound sympathetic connection to the rest of the life on Earth. Ecstatic mysticism is content merely to touch God, and

ABOVE: **Enlightenment, the goal of all mystic study and exercise, is a blissful wellspring of joy and contentment in the simplest of moments.**

is less concerned with deeper knowledge of his blueprints and plans for the universe, although it does bring the wisdom of clear sight.

One of the most common mistakes is to assume that bliss is a passive state. Some people are concerned that if they feel deeply fulfilled, happy and at peace, then they will not have any motivation to actually ever get off their backsides and do anything. The term "Lotus-eater," meaning someone too complacent to recognize impending trouble or danger, is a direct reference back to misconceptions about Buddhist monks. In fact, nothing could be further from the truth. Experiencing a sense of bliss is like waking up in a really good mood – it makes you want to bounce up and get involved in the day – with the added bonus that you feel at peace with yourself and everybody else. You only want to stay in bed and do nothing if you wake up feeling depressed or scared.

Another common mistake is the belief that the journey down the mystical path somehow changes your personality, turning you into a "New-Age Guru" type. While the path does require some self-improvement, it is a process that involves becoming more yourself, not less. The road teaches you to put aside the old fears and pains that warp you as a person, shows you how to avoid compulsions that have caused you problems, and, in the end, teaches you on a direct, experiential level that all life is one and is worthy of love and respect. None of this will modify who you truly are. On the contrary, the path is about discovering who you would have been if your life to date had been perfect for your developmental needs – it is about clearing away the debris from around your soul and

allowing it to blossom. In this respect, the mystic path is like therapy – it helps exorcise old ghosts and demons, and gives you confidence in yourself.

Another misunderstanding is that there is something inherently magical about the mystic path – either that it is somehow supernatural, or that it is some sort of mock-occult claptrap used to con the foolish out of large amounts of money. The mystical path is entirely natural – a way of connecting to the spark of life-force within ourselves and, through it, to the spark within everyone else too. It involves finding a wellspring of peace and happiness within yourself. There is nothing occult or supernatural about that. What could be more wonderful than spending the rest of your life feeling really happy? With everything else pared away, that is the essence of the mystic path. Sadly, there are always people willing to prey on others, and there is no shortage of thieves pretending to sell mystic wisdom, In general, successful mystics are not interested in accumulating large amounts of wealth.

Less commonly, some people have concerns about the safety of the mystical path. If it is undertaken properly – that is, patiently – then there is no danger. By working meditatively with the Sephiroth and Nativoth, the aspirant (literally, "one who hopes") allows the deeper parts of the mind to shape the meditational experiences. Meditation rarely goes exactly as foreseen – in fact, if nothing unplanned occurs, that is usually a sign that the meditation has stayed on a very superficial level, with little connection to the unconscious. Typical indications of a successful meditation include meeting (and communicating with) various beings, finding certain pathways blocked, being shown images that relate to imbalances that need correcting, and so on. For example, the Great Library of Hod should be teeming with students, librarians and researchers when the aspirant connects with it. If it is empty, or the books inside are blank or impossible to read, then that is a sure sign that the meditation has not made a true connection with the deeper mind. When a strong link is made, the aspirant is able to talk to the other seekers inside, browse through the books, ask librarians for guidance, and so on. It may take several attempts to make the first good connection to any given sphere or path.

Providing that the aspirant is guided by meditations, and works with the imagery thrown up by the mind, then there is no possible danger. The only risks occur when the aspirant is impatient, forcing a way through the paths without dedicating proper time to meet the challenges posed by each sphere, or to properly answer the questions it asks. Reckless ascent can lead the aspirant

BELOW: **This Renaissance library with its book-filled alcoves and niches is reminiscent of the Great Library of Hod.**

to the abyss too quickly, resulting (at the worst) in new neurotic obsessions. However, it takes a certain amount of work along the path to actually have a chance of connecting with the abyss, so even that danger is comparatively small.

Toward Enlightenment

There are four main paths to enlightenment up the Tree of Life. They are known as the left-hand path, the right-hand path, the path of the arrow and the path of the sword. The most common choice of western aspirants is the path of the sword. It gets its name from the path it traces, in descending numerical order, through the ten Sephiroth, like a jagged sword slash. The path of the sword requires the aspirant to work with each sphere (and the paths leading up to it) in turn, until the energies of that sphere are balanced, and free of psychological blockage and debris. The three pairs of linked spheres also have to be balanced with each other.

In addition to working with each Sephiroth in turn, most aspirants on the path of the sword also perform a meditative exercise called "Rising Through the Spheres" once or twice a month. As it sounds, this is a long meditation in which the aspirant passes through each Sephira in turn, spending a short time in each to call upon the divine names and energies within than sphere. At Binah (or sometimes Chokmah) the aspirant then descends back the same way, clothing herself in the pure mantle of each sphere in turn. This helps her attune to the Tree in general, and smoothes the path ahead.

The path of the sword is popular because it does not require any great alterations to lifestyle. If the aspirant works with just one sphere at any one time, the impact on everyday life is reduced. This route is the closest to western-style therapy in feel, in that it involves an extended, and sequential, process of self-examination on different aspects of life. Time taken to walk the path varies from individual to individual. It depends on their commitment to, and capacity for, personal change, their state of spiritual and psychological health, and so on. On average, an aspirant should aim to spend a minimum of

an hour or so in meditation three times a week and also practise the exercises associated with the relevant sphere (listed in Chapter Four) three times a week. If this is attainable, then 18-36 months will be spent on the path – that is, an average of two to four weeks working on each of the Sephiroth and Nativoth.

The path of the arrow is the usual choice of cloistered aspirants, and others who are able to withdraw totally from the world and devote themselves to the spiritual for a time. It gets its name from the straight line it blazes up the tree, from Malkuth, through Tiphareth, to Kether. It is a path of spiritual purification, of refining the consciousness from the material to the divine. It is a much faster route than the path of the sword, but it is also more arduous, and more prone to failure. To have a good chance of success, aspirants really need the assistance of a teacher who has taken the route already.

It is expected that aspirants on the path of the arrow will balance the pillars of severity and mercy within themselves as part of their progress up the middle pillar.

Spiritual purity can only be achieved through balance. All of the aspirant's time is devoted to purification rituals, prayer, meditation and other devotional activities. The aim is to effectively bring Malkuth and Yesod in line with Tiphareth, and then bring all three in line with Kether, making progress up the tree possible. The successful aspirant is almost drawn over the abyss automatically as holiness increases. As before, the time taken is highly variable, but a student concentrating on nothing but the path of the arrow may complete the journey in as little as six months.

The left-hand and right-hand paths are traditionally associated more with theurgical (supernatural) mysticism than with ecstatic – in other words, they are chosen more by aspirants who start off seeking power. They correspond to black and white magic respectively, and typically

LEFT: **Meditation can be incorporated into a busy schedule to refresh the soul, even in a hectic place.**

BELOW: **The Native American bear dance, led by a shaman in bear furs, was used to raise energy for the shaman to contact and channel the blessings of Bear, the totem spirit – primarily of protection and healing.**

take several years to master, because the aspirant is after more than just enlightenment.

The right-hand path is the path of energy and compassion. The idea is to rise through the tree by increasing personal energy levels rather than through a process of refinement. There are a number of techniques for increasing one's spiritual energy on a short-term basis – concentration, meditation, yoga, sex, dancing, drumming, drugs and so on – and some, or all, are commonly used. Through the assistance of relevant guided meditation and other exercises, the energy is channelled into raising the consciousness out of Malkuth and up through the Pillar of Mercy. This is experienced physically as progress of energy from the base of the spine to the top of the head, as in the *Kundalini* serpent of tantra. As the consciousness expands, so does the awareness that the self is kin to all that is.

Progress along the path is marked by the maximum levels of spiritual energy that can be attained. Eventually, the aspirant bursts out onto the abyss with sufficient energy to be pushed across, and into, the limitless energy and awareness of Chokmah. The theoretical power that the path provides lies in the spare energy that it generates for the aspirant.

The left-hand path is effectively opposite to the right-hand path. The aspirant strips away all emotion and attachment from the self, and seeks to still the pieces that remain. In this manner, the energy required to penetrate Binah is negligible. This path is the most corrosive on the personality of all the main options, for it requires that all connections, desires and morals must be sacrificed in the name of pure will. It is only when the left-hand aspirant is capable of any act that the remaining will is light enough to resist sinking into the abyss.

Historically, some left-hand mystics have sought to scourge themselves of unwanted attachment by sinking to some quite spectacular depravities, which is why the path has such a bad name. That is one of the path's traps, however, and will lead the aspirant straight through the abyss and into the Qliphoth – pure will does not require depravity or malice. It is lonely and isolated, but successful progress most definitely does not require blood sacrifices. The left-hand path still leads to the same end as all other paths – unity, bliss and compassion. The power that it supposedly offers is that of diamond-hard, unyielding will.

BELOW: **A group of alchemists demonstrate a magical serum in the classic painting from 1757, "The Alchemists" by Pietro Longhi.**

The Alchemical Tradition

Alchemy is usually thought of as an early form of chemistry that centred on the search for the Philosopher's Stone – a substance that would turn lead into gold and grant eternal youth. Other historical goals of alchemy have included the Sovereign Remedy, which would heal all illnesses; Greek Fire, a substance akin to modern napalm; and Aqua Regia, an acid so powerful that it would eat through any substance.

It is a matter of simple fact that many alchemists over the last 3,000 years have indeed devoted a huge amount of time and effort to attaining these goals, particularly the chemical creation of gold. It seems silly to us now, but until modern science proved the vast difficulties of altering one element into another, there was no reason for learned sages to assume that it was beyond them. With the right set of chemicals and substances and the correct procedures they believed that wealth or immortality was within their grasp.

At the same time, however, it is clear that right from its earliest beginnings, alchemy has had a spiritual component. On all levels, alchemy is about purification – the transformation of that which is common into an incorruptible spiritual version. Gold is the symbol of that purity, partly because of its value, and partly because of its qualities and non-reactive nature. Similarly, the eternal life of the Philosopher's Stone is that of the pure, enlightened soul. Alchemy's metaphor for spiritual purity is rate of vibration: the more highly purified the substance (or soul) is, the higher its vibration rate. In the alchemical tradition, creation of the Philosopher's Stone should be seen as a benchmark – an indication that the alchemist has purified himself sufficiently to gain power over many of Nature's secrets. The parallels to Kabbalistic mysticism are plain.

Alchemy's precise origins are uncertain. One popular theory is that the term derives from Khem, the name that the ancient Egyptians gave to their country, suggesting that the art was originally Egyptian. Other scholars believe that the word (and art) is derived from ancient Greek. Others believe that, like much of modern chemistry, alchemy arose in dynastic China, or that it developed in India in the Vedic sciences, or in the Middle East. Wherever it first developed, alchemy is certainly close to 3,000 years old, and has been practised in various forms in all of the above places.

In recent years, plenty of researchers have been quick to seize on one aspect of alchemy and deny the other entirely. Certainly, some dedicated alchemists were also early scientists – Paracelsus and Isaac Newton are two of the best known alchemists, and are generally considered the founders of medicine and physics respectively. On the other hand, several psychologists and philosophers have looked at historical alchemy and assumed that the entire procedure was an elaborate metaphor for

Aureolus Philippus Theophrastus Paracelsus
ex Familia Brombastorum ab Hohenheim
Philosophus, Medicus, Mathematicus Chimist
Cabalista, rerum naturæ industrius, indagator
Alterius non fit, qui suus esse potest * Laus Deo
Pax vivis, Requies æterna sepultis.

RIGHT: **Aurelius Philippus Paracelsus of Hohenheim, a scientist, philosopher and alchemist, is shown here with a work on the Kabbalah ready by his side.**

ABOVE: **The energies of creation pour out onto the landscape and are collected in dew trays in this highly symbolic and allegorical alchemical teaching illustration.**

base technique used for refining both substances and the psyche itself, the route to creating a unified, balanced whole. Substances (and people) were thought to be made up of the four elements; fire, air, water and earth. These were expressed through the medium of the three principal substances, salt, sulphur and mercury. As the energy of life passes through the elements, it takes on the characteristics that will give it form in the real world. This energy is the *Prima Materia*, which is called Chaos in the Bible. It is the point where duality has become complete, and energy becomes both active and passive. In the image of the *Golden Chain of Homer*, the active principle is called niter and the passive is salt. The active energy manifests as fire and air, and is identified with sulphur, the soul of a thing. The passive energy manifests as water and earth, and is identified with salt, the physical body of a thing. The third principle, mercury, is air and water, the junction between the two pairs which makes transmission possible and is identified as the general life force.

Correspondences to the Tree of Life are clear. The *Solve et Coagula* is an elegant recreation of the doctrine of the Sundering – having been split, the energy of the divine must be purified and then put back together again to usher in the golden age. The four elements correspond directly to the four worlds of existence. Fire is Atziluth, the first cause of pure energy. Air is Briah, where archetypes start to take form. Water is Yetzirah, the fluid world of the astral and psychic. Finally, Earth is Assiah, the solid realm of reality. The three principles correspond to the pillars of the tree. Salt, the passive principle, is the Pillar of Severity. Sulphur, being active, is the Pillar of Mercy. Mercury, which is the interface and balanced point, the representative of life force, is the middle Pillar of Balance. The *Prima Materia* is the shard of the divine itself, God's force within.

self-improvement. Both Carl Jung and Israel Regardie made that mistake, although Regardie later learnt of alchemy's laboratory tradition and came to express a belief that it was based in natural and demonstrable laws.

The principles of alchemy show clear correspondences to Kabbalistic thought. The core process of alchemy is summarized by the Latin phrase "*Solve et Coagula*" – "separate, purify and recombine." This is the

There is no room to go into further detail on the correspondences between alchemy and the Kabbalah, but the links are strong and deep. It is very easy to perceive alchemy as an alternate way of expressing the wisdom of the Kabbalah. This is not surprising, considering the prominence of Kabbalism during the alchemical heyday of the fifteenth and sixteenth centuries.

The History of the Tarot

Traditional playing cards first arrived in Europe from the Middle East in AD 1376. The first ever references to cards date from 1377, and they appear in new laws forbidding gambling, reported religious sermons, books about gaming, and so on. Playing cards established a firm hold right across Europe. Approximately 50 years later, in northern Italy, they gave birth to the first forerunners of the tarot.

The earliest forms of the tarot were called triumph cards. References to them start appearing in recorded literature as early as 1420 (as the game of "Gods and Birds"), clearly differentiating packs of triumph cards from packs of standard playing cards. The earliest triumph cards themselves have been dated to the lifetime of Duke Visconti of Milan, who held power there from 1412 to 1447. Researchers have ascertained that by the end of the fifteenth century, some 50 years later, triumph cards were being made in Milan, Venice, Florence, Bologna and Ferrara. Triumph card decks included a set of allegorical art cards that were considered to "triumph over" (or "trump") normal cards, and they had a specific ranking order of their own. The cards spread to France early in the sixteenth century.

The name *Tarocchi* appears for the first time around 1530. Card players had discovered that you could play triumphs with ordinary cards by designating one of the four suits as the triumphant (trump) suit – the start of the game of Bridge. "Triumph" became an ambiguous term, and specific triumph card decks needed a new name. The reasons behind the term they chose remain uncertain, but Tarocchi is certainly the origin of the French term "tarot."

RIGHT: **This Tarocchi triumph card depicting the devil is only about 100 years old, but the illustration is a faithful recollection of very early Tarocchi cards.**

There was a fair amount of variation among early triumph decks. The symbols of the tarot trumps that we know today are all found among the artistic symbolism of the Italian Renaissance, and no source other than the triumph decks has survived to suggest a collection of these archetypal images.

It is possible that the earliest triumph deck was inspired by Duke Visconti himself. There are records of the young duke directing his tutor, the court astrologer Marziano da Tortona, to come up with a card game. Visconti wanted the ordinary suits of the playing cards to be replaced with suits representing virtues, riches, virginities and pleasures. Each suit was to additionally have four cards higher than its four court cards, and the new cards would depict classical deities. The sixteen deities influenced each other in an internal order that ignored suit assignments.

The commission for the cards was passed to a local artistic genius, Michelino da Besozzo, who apparently created a deck of incredible beauty. In the meantime, Marziano prepared a book to go with the cards that described the deities, how they were depicted, and what each one represented. The book, which still exists, in the Bibliotheque Nationale in Paris, France, does not even give card game rules, focusing entirely on the allegories behind the images of the cards and their correct ranking.

The modern configuration of the tarot nowadays is to have 22 trump cards in the Major Arcana, and 56 cards in the suits of the Minor Arcana. Each of the four suits is split into cards numbered 1–10 and then four further "court" cards of increasing rank. This structure is known to be the same as the "Tarocchi of Venice" deck (also called the Lombardi deck), after an example of the Venetian/Piedmontese triumphs.

We do not know exactly who created the version of triumphs that became the standard tarot that we know today. However, given the strength of the Kabbalah at that period – particularly its influence in Italy late in the fifteenth century – a greater or lesser degree of cross-fertilization seems certain. This is particularly evident in the numerical parallels between the tarot and the Tree and the foundation of the triumphs in the fifteenth century as the allegory-rich work of a learned astrologer and sage.

The Tarot and the Tree

The tarot first gained mass-market popularity with a sixteenth-century deck known as the Tarot de Marseille, which had the great bonus of arriving just in time for commercial printing to make it cheaply available. It was still considered a game at the time, albeit one that was rich in symbolism and allegory. Esoteric analysis of the cards really began to take off in the 1700s, once the dark oppression of the Inquisition and the witch trials had died down. Alchemy, ritual magic and divination were all common interests among the learned, and study of the Kabbalah went hand in hand with all three.

Eliphas Levi was not the first researcher to suggest the link between the Tree of Life and the tarot; the idea had been around for almost 150 years. It was Levi, however, who really formalized the idea. His work on the

ABOVE: **Tarot de Marseille, the oldest deck in production.**

RIGHT: **The devil – as revealed by Eliphas Levi in "Transcendental Magic."**

ABOVE: **The Rider-Waite tarot deck, from which these Tarot trumps come, was devised along highly Kabbalistic lines.**

subject was detailed and thorough, and convinced the general occult community enough for the model to become the dominant system of interpreting the structure of the tarot. Levi himself was convinced that the tarot had been devised from Kabbalistic principles, although he never claimed to have actual historical proof. Some other thinkers have taken the startling parallels between the Tree and the tarot as proof of the universality. This author believes that the Kabbalah did have an influence in the tarot's final design, along with several other areas of arcane, scientific and artistic knowledge.

During the great occult revival at the end of the ninteenth century, the tarot went through a significant period of development. Levi's work was adopted enthusiastically by the Golden Dawn, and its members contributed significantly to the development of some of the most influential modern decks around, as well as advancing the understanding and symbology of the subject. Most of the enduring associations between the tarot and other magical systems were created by the Golden Dawn's enthusiastic syncretism.

Arguably the two greatest tarot decks in use today are the Rider-Waite tarot and the Book of Thoth. Both were created by Golden Dawn members, drawing explicitly on significant amounts of imagery and teachings from the Kabbalah. The Rider-Waite tarot was created by Arthur Edward Waite in the first decade of the twentieth century. Waite was one of the foremost initiates of the Golden

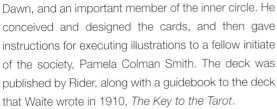

Dawn, and an important member of the inner circle. He conceived and designed the cards, and then gave instructions for executing illustrations to a fellow initiate of the society, Pamela Colman Smith. The deck was published by Rider, along with a guidebook to the deck that Waite wrote in 1910, *The Key to the Tarot*.

The Book of Thoth was designed by the infamous Golden Dawn star Aleister Crowley. He originally estimated that it would take three months to develop, but in the end design work on the deck – which contained several major deviations from standard tarot templates – lasted from 1938 to 1943. The illustrations were painted by a friend of Crowley's, Lady Frieda Harris. Crowley then used his deck to illuminate a book about the tarot, also called the *Book of Thoth*, which he published in 1944. The deck itself remained private, and did not see publi-

cation until after both Crowley's and Harris's deaths, in 1969. Crowley's deck remains controversial for its deviations. Some researchers feel that his work corrects several earlier mistakes in correspondence with the Tree of Life and the orthodox Kabbalah, while others point out his notorious sense of humour, and argue that some of the changes are jokes or traps inserted to test the worthiness of the user.

Both the Rider-Waite tarot and the Book of Thoth are crammed full of Kabbalistic, astrological, alchemical and magical symbolism. While they retain the important symbolic aspects of other decks, they have several extra layers of meaning and significance as well. Crowley's deck is particularly rich, as each card of the Minor Arcana contains its own fully-developed picture and esoteric title. The Rider-Waite and the Thoth are still the two best-

LEFT: **A Golden Dawn illustration of the Kabbalistic Cross with its allegorical three pillars of the Tree of Life.**

RIGHT: **Aleister Crowley and his soulmate Leah Hirsig at their Sicilian villa in 1921. Mussolini expelled them in 1923 after a disciple, Raoul Loveday, died from drinking cat's blood.**

respected tarot decks available today. The Thoth is generally held to retain something of the personality of its creator, being frank to the point of brutality, and having a rather piquant sense of humour. The Rider-Waite, by comparison, is considered steady and even-tempered, but somewhat unadventurous.

The parallels between the Tree of Life and the tarot are out in the open. The Tree has ten Sephiroth, each of which exists in the four worlds of creation. Likewise, the tarot has ten numbered Minor Arcana cards for each of the four suits. The ten Sephiroth can further be divided up into four groups to represent the worlds – on each of the four instances of the Tree. Likewise, the tarot's Minor Arcana has four court cards – in each suit. The 22 Nativoth of the Tree connect the Sephiroth together. Likewise, the 22 Major Arcana illuminate the minor cards.

The trumps are usually attributed to the Tree in order, starting with the Fool as 0, so that Nativa 11, Aleph, is the Fool (Trump 0) and 12, Beth, is the Magician (Trump 1). This runs down to 32, Tau, as the Universe (Trump 21). The Minor Arcana also follow the tree by number – the aces of each suit correspond to Kether and run through to the 10s of each suit corresponding to Malkuth. Other attributions follow elemental lines:

Suit	Court Card	World	Element	Tree Portion
Pentacles	Page	Assiah	Earth	Malkuth
Swords	Knight	Yetzirah	Air	Tiphareth & surrounding spheres
Cups	Queen	Briah	Water	Binah
Wands	King	Aztiluth	Fire	Chokmah & Kether

When it comes to interpretation and comparative understanding, each card of the Major Arcana indicates the nature of the relationship between the two Sephiroth linked by the associated path. For example, Trump 13, Death, is associated with the path linking Netzach to Tiphareth. Death, as a tarot card, represents transformation and refinement; the path of Nun is likewise the path of transformation, along which the self of the personality finally makes contact with the Self of the immortal soul. Similarly, the Minor Arcana of each suit for a given number correspond to that Sephira, expressing its energy as part of the manifest world (pentacles), the formative world of intellect (swords), the receptive world of emotion (cups) or the creative world (fire).

Deep study of the interrelations between the modern tarot and the Tree of Life is extremely rewarding, and can greatly increase understanding of both fields. It can also be a great help in evoking appropriate imagery during meditations along the paths of the Tree.

Living with the Kabbalah

The Kabbalah still has a vast amount to offer the modern world. Its teachings are particularly valuable in troubled times like these, when life seems to have lost meaning and direction for so many people. Interest in the Kabbalah has never been stronger, even during the Renaissance of the fifteenth and sixteenth centuries. The Tree of Life has put down roots within the western mystery tradition, and grown to become the very heart of it. Small wonder then that people from all walks of life are turning to its mysteries, and that the mass media are taking notice.

A Troubled World

The modern world is in a state of crisis. While a few mega-rich increase their fortunes by billions every year, the rest of us are finding it harder and harder to make ends meet. Jobs are coming under increasing pressure, hours are getting longer, holiday time is shrinking and stress is mounting, but salaries are staying the same at best – and meanwhile, the cost of living is rising steadily. Provisions for old age that looked great 20 years ago now seem frighteningly inadequate, and the young face the possibility of not being able to retire until the age of 75 just to be certain of making ends meet. Acceptable education is increasingly becoming the privilege of the rich.

Meanwhile, out in the wider world, we have climate change, pollution, medicine-resistant super-diseases and constant warfare – the planet has not known a single day of peace in the last 50 years. Even the oil industry's paid scientists and apologists can no longer argue that global warming is not occurring; their only defence is to argue that it is happening because of natural causes, not as the result of the toxic gases that are being spewed into the atmosphere. Meanwhile the weather is becoming more and more unpredictable. The public are being kept in a constant state of terror thanks to the incessant barrage of fear from news sources and governments. Public and private sector debts are through the roof. House prices and the stock market are so inflated that another depres-

sion seems unavoidable. Oil is hitting crisis-level prices. Everywhere you turn, you see glossy adverts for merchandise that you cannot afford and don't need but are made to feel you must have in order to prove successful.

The stress that we are all under is utterly unprecedented in the world's history. We are isolated, scared and pushed so hard that we hardly have time to talk to our nearest and dearest like human beings. Even our television entertainment is mostly made up of scenes of violence, pain and humiliation masquerading as "reality." It is no way to live, and we all know it; the best we can say is that we are a lot better off than the four-fifths of the world stuck below the poverty line, desperately scrabbling for scraps to eat. That our great-great-grandfathers put them there in the first place just adds to the stress.

With all this endemic pain and pressure, it is no surprise that most of us feel hollow and unfulfilled. We long for peace, ease and happiness. The Kabbalah has lessons that can help all of us. It gives us a way to bring ourselves into balance, lets us see some of the structure that underlies the world, and provides us with a set of tools which we can use to start working toward inner peace. For those with the inclination, it lays out a perfectly straightforward path toward genuine spiritual fulfilment.

OPPOSITE: **Madonna Ciccone is one of the most famous students of Kabbalah – and certainly its longest-standing, high-profile adherent.**

Finding Out More about Kabbalah

The Kabbalah has been attracting a lot of attention in the mass media recently. The key that sparked a recent round of interest and speculation was Madonna's sensational July revelation on the *20/20 News Show* that she had changed her name to "Esther." Madonna said that she wanted to attach herself to the energies of a different name, one more in tune with her Kabbalistic study. As she was originally named after her mother, she also wanted to get away from the energies of the cancer that claimed her mother's life early on. Madonna has actually been studying the Kabbalah for several years now and is a dedicated student by anyone's standards.

BELOW: **Britney Spears is a recent convert to Kabbalistic study. Note the red cord of Rachel tied around her left wrist.**

Much has been written in the mainstream press and in Jewish circles about various high-profile Kabbalah training organisations and their leaders. Some are seen as little more than mock-Kabbalistic money-siphoning cults, while others are reputed to be genuine places of miracle. Which are which depends on who you ask, of course.

The controversy surrounding the whole area has done little to dampen celebrity interest. A long list of stars has been linked to the study of the Kabbalah, from established figures such as Elizabeth Taylor, Donna Karan, Demi Moore, Winona Ryder and Kirk Douglas to newcomers such as Britney Spears, Lindsay Lohan and Paris Hilton.

Traditional Israelite amulets are even starting to become fashionable in celebrity circles. The most famous is the red cord of Rachel. These blessed red-string bracelets are traditionally supposed to represent an umbilical link between the wearer and the biblical heroine, and to fend off all manner of malignant energies. It used to be that the best place to find authentic red cord amulets was from the wise-women clustered around the Wailing Wall in Jerusalem, but as mainstream interest in the Kabbalah has grown, so has availability.

There are many good, reliable Kabbalah teachers around the world. If you are interested in learning more about the Kabbalah, we have provided a starting list of resources at the end of the book. Just remember that a group may be popular or receive a lot of celebrity interest and not necessarily be the best source of enlightenment for you. Ask yourself, how many celebrities are known for their spiritual wisdom?

If you are looking for guidance and teaching, you should conduct extensive research on all would-be teachers via the Internet – and that includes the people and places listed in our Resources section. Always do your research carefully, and, most of all, remember what the Baal Shem Tov said about telling teachers from charlatans:

"Ask the teacher if he knows how to banish machshavot ra'ot, the evil thoughts. If he says he has the secret, then he is a fraud."

Practical Lessons from the Tree

There are many ways that you can integrate the Kabbalah into your daily life to make positive changes. One of the most obvious is also the simplest – try to live your life in a manner that is true to the spheres of the Tree. There are no ten Kabbalistic commandments, but each of the Sephiroth has a message and an energy that you can integrate into your life.

Kether reminds you that you are part of God's limitless love, and asks you to act from that position. Binah and Chokmah, when balanced, remind you to act always with compassion and to do unto others as you would do unto yourself, for we are all one. Chesed and Geburah teach generosity and kindness, but also remind you that sometimes the kindest thing to do is to say "No," turn around and walk away. Tiphareth asks you to be true to your inner self, and to have faith and confidence in yourself. Netzach and Hod require you to have awareness of your feelings and accept them for what they are. Yesod reminds you that the monsters in your mind, remembered or imagined, should not restrict you. Malkuth, finally, has the most salient message of all: this is your life, right here, right now, and it is yours to make the most of. If you don't, no one will.

On a more specific basis, there are exercises from cultures and systems all over the world that you can use to heighten your connections with each of the spheres, and to strengthen yourself in the areas that they represent. Each one has value to offer you on several levels. You should make notes during any programme of exercise, physical, mental, or spiritual, as a matter of course. It is particularly important that you keep a record of any Kabbalistic exercises or meditations you do. Remember to include records of how you did, how you felt before and after, and whether you experienced anything unexpected during the session. If you visit the Sephiroth or Nativoth meditatively, then always write down as much detail as you can afterward – all sorts of details may prove significant at a later date. Any time you're feeling down about your progress with an exercise, read back over your earliest notes for it and see how you have progressed. You'll be amazed.

The Five Senses Exercise

SPHERE: *Malkuth*
BENEFITS: *Physical grounding, calming, connection to Malkuth energies*
FREQUENCY: *Two to three times weekly*
DURATION: *Three weeks*
MAINTENANCE: *The standard exercise when you are feeling disconnected from the world*

You need to assemble a few simple items for this exercise – specifically, a picture of something that you feel strongly about, positively or negatively; a small amount of flavoursome food or drink; something scented; and something with a texture that you can feel easily.

Before you begin, put your items in front of you and make sure you won't be disturbed for five minutes. Close your eyes and breathe slowly and deeply for a few moments, breathing in for the count of four, holding a beat, and then breathing out again for the count of four. After several slow breaths, open your eyes.

Pick up the picture and look at it. Consider the subject. Think about how it makes you feel. Remember a few facts associated with the subject, and previous occasions in the past when you have been particularly aware of the subject. Try to be aware of all your mental activity associated with looking at the picture.

Now close your eyes, and tell yourself: "None of this is Malkuth." Open them again and look back at the picture. This time, make a special effort to ignore what it is about. Just look at the play of light and shadow, line and definition, colour and form, and do your best to ignore its overall meaning. Tell yourself: "This is Malkuth."

Now repeat the process for your other four senses. You have objects ready for taste, smell and touch; for sound, use your hands to clap a musical rhythm or knock a familiar door-knock pattern on a table. In each instance, the first thing you should do is to make the most of the experience as a conscious event, linked to your thoughts, feelings and memories. Then remind

ABOVE: **Immerse yourself in the world of your senses and let your worries and concerns of past and future just fade away.**

yourself that such things are not of Malkuth, and repeat the experience. The second time, focus entirely on your sensory input, and switch as much of your mind off as you can.

You only need to perform this exercise a few times to really strengthen your understanding of, and connection to, Malkuth. It is the sphere that we live in the most, and so it is the easiest for us to access. You can repeat the exercise any time you're feeling disconnected from reality, or you feel that mental or emotional concerns are weighing you down and you want to get back to "keeping it real."

Za Zen

SPHERE: *Malkuth*

BENEFITS: *Vital for success in many later exercises, reduces stress, refreshes mind*

FREQUENCY: *Daily*

DURATION: *Four weeks or more*

MAINTENANCE: *Standard exercise at least once a week*

The Za Zen is the Buddhist "No mind" meditation. It requires no preparation, and is extremely simple in principle. Make sure you won't be disturbed for five minutes, sit down comfortably, close your eyes and take several slow, deep breaths as described above. Now, continuing to breathe slowly and easily, silence your mind. We all vocalize thoughts almost all the time; make a conscious effort to stop. Clear all mental images from your mind's eye. If you are imagining any sounds, get rid of those too. It will require an act of concentration to cease

any one of the three; initially, you may have to actively invoke silence by picturing blankness, speaking spaces to yourself (" ......"), and so on. Thoughts and images will intrude, almost immediately. Accept that they have done so, and banish them again. Do not allow yourself to react mentally or emotionally to them.

Don't expect too much from yourself. For the first week or two, even managing to get a second's mental silence over the course of a five-minute session is a major victory. You will get better, however – and your record will be a vital aid in keeping your morale up. Vocalized thoughts such as "Wow! Four seconds! I'm doing great!" are particularly irritating. When you can still your mind for five to ten seconds at a time, advance to doing the practice with your eyes open or, if you want a real challenge, out in public in a busy setting. If you have the time in your schedule, keep practising daily until you can keep your mind quiet indefinitely. It sounds nearly impossible, I know, but once you can do a ten-second stretch, complete silence follows fairly easily.

LEFT: **The inner dialogue of vocalized thought that plagues us constantly is a compound of fears, guilts and old defeats. In its silence, you will find power.**

As well as giving your mind a much-needed break and refreshing you on several different levels, the Za Zen meditation is a vital prerequisite for some of the later exercises. It is the only weapon you have at your disposal when you want to make sure that your conscious or subconscious minds are not cluttering up your meditations and other exercises with static. It also helps build willpower, calms and relaxes you, and once you get good at it, provides you with ready access to the pure state of Malkuth – experience without mentation.

Visualization

SPHERE: *Yesod*

BENEFITS: *Link to Yesod, strengthens imagina-tion, improves rapport with unconscious, vital for many later exercises*

FREQUENCY: *Daily*

DURATION: *Contingent on progress*

MAINTENANCE: *Standard exercise at least once a week*

Visualization is the art of training yourself to see images vividly in your mind's eye. As such, it is one of the most important skills you can develop for future work with the Tree, because it will make your meditations significantly clearer and more absorbing. It requires no preparation. Make sure you're not going to be disturbed for five minutes and make yourself comfortable physically, sitting or lying down as you prefer. Close your eyes and take several slow, deep breaths. Concentrate on your

mind's eye, and imagine the number "2." Picture it in your mind's eye, in white, as if it was written in chalk on a black-board. Just concentrate on it, and keep it in mind.

When you feel that you have a fairly firm mental hold on it, add another digit next to it. You can pick one at random, or select digits from a number that has meaning to you, like your telephone number. Remembering to keep the "2" vivid, hold the second number next to it. When it is stabilized, add another number, and then another, and keep going until you can no longer hold the whole number simultaneously in your mind's eye. At that point, start back from the first "2," and try building back up.

During your first attempts, you may find that even the initial "2" is wavering and difficult to retain. That's perfectly normal; visualization is not something that many of us practise. Keep at it, and you'll find that you quickly improve. When you can hold an entire ten-digit phone number steady for minutes at a time, expand your horizons a little. Imagine the surface of your mind's eye really is a blackboard, complete with chalk dust and a wooden frame. Rub a number out and replace it with something else. Fill in the rest of the classroom that the blackboard is in. Finally populate it with attentive, polite, quiet little children.

If you can hold the image of an entire class – with individual children in specific places – and still retain the numbers you started with, then you've mastered visual-ization. You can move on earlier though if you are impatient to give up visualization training, but make sure you can at least envision the blackboard and the wall it is mounted on. This is likely to take several weeks.

You'll find that visualization is easier some days than others. Factors such as fatigue, when you last ate and even the moon's phase may play a role. Look back over your notes and see what correspondences you can identify. As well as the critical benefits your meditations will receive from a well-trained visualizing ability, be aware that when you work with images in your mind's eye, you are painting pictures with the very fabric of Yesod itself. It is the essence of everything that Yesod is.

LEFT: **Visualization is the key to successful meditation. The better you are at it, the greater your results elsewhere.**

Cascading

SPHERE: *Yesod*

BENEFITS: *Taps into unconscious wells of creativity and knowledge, can help solve any problem*

FREQUENCY: *Daily*

DURATION: *A month*

MAINTENANCE: *Five-minute top-up weekly*

For the best results with this exercise, you need a Dictaphone or tape recorder. If something of the sort isn't available then you can go without, but you'll blunt the effectiveness of your practice sessions quite seriously. Go somewhere you feel comfortable talking to yourself out loud. Start the recorder, close your eyes and imagine yourself in a room. Start describing the room you are imagining, out loud, in as much detail as you can muster. Don't let yourself stop talking for any more than an instant or the amount of time it takes to draw a quick breath. Speak quickly. If you find yourself hesitating or pausing, just say the first thing that comes into your mind.

When there's nothing more in the room for you to describe, turn your attention outside the room – head out of the door, look out of the window. Keep describing everything you imagine. Don't try to guide the images, and don't think about what you are saying. Do your best to just connect your mouth to your imagination, and let it run. Move through your imaginary landscape however you see fit. Leap out of windows and fly, if you want to. It's all in your mind. Just don't try to censor or predict what you are going to encounter, and keep talking about it. If any other thought occurs to you in the meantime, blurt it out. If the landscape shifts suddenly, roll with it. Your only job is to keep your mouth fed with words.

For the first week, just keep the cascade going for five minutes. You'll find that your mind resists you at first; and you'll spend a lot of time saying "ummmm uhhhh ummmm" or cursing repeatedly as you try to find words.

RIGHT: **Never underestimate your unconscious. Cascading can give you the best answers to every single question that torments you.**

This is to be expected. You will improve. Make a point of listening to the tape you make a couple of hours later. You may find interesting points or bits of imagery that have a bearing on your current life situation, or that draw parallels with problems you are having. By listening back over it, you'll also help reinforce yourself against big gaps in your speech, or lots of umming and ahhing. Write your notes each day after listening back over the tape, and remember to jot down anything that seems out of place or grabs your interest. After the first week, increase to ten minutes and then again to 15 minutes for weeks three and four.

You can use cascading as a practical tool as well as a general exercise. If you have a problem, a difficult situation, a puzzling question or a creative challenge that is giving you some trouble, cascading can solve it for you. Before you start the session, think of a physical object that can represent the problem. Just before you close your eyes, say "I am going to come up with great

solutions to my problem of <…describe the problem…>." Then when you start cascading, begin by describing the object, and then a room that you might typically find it in. Pay particular attention to other objects in the room, or the territory outside the door. Recording will prove particularly important here because you won't remember everything you say – maybe not even half of it – and you may miss vital clues to solving the trouble.

Go back over the tape slowly afterward, and consider how the symbolism of things you mention in the cascade can help answer the question. Your unconscious mind is very creative and eager to help when you pay it attention, and I have never known cascading to fail to come up with innovative options. This is particularly true later in the cascade, so if you can keep it going for 20 or 30 minutes to work on a problem, so much the better.

Brainstorming

SPHERE: *Hod*

BENEFITS: *Connection to Hod, good for coming up with ideas*

FREQUENCY: *Two to three times weekly*

DURATION: *Ten sessions*

MAINTENANCE: *Full session on a particular issue as required*

You'll need a large piece of paper and a pen, and ideally a desk to work at. You can brainstorm on any topic, but for the purposes of this exercise we're going to use the Sephiroth. Select one of the Sephiroth, and write its name at the top of the paper. Then write down a list of qualities that you think the Sephira embodies or possesses, along with any life situations or specific settings or images that you think really embody that Sephira. In other words, write down every possible answer to the question "What does Sephira X mean to me?"

While you're brainstorming, don't try to censor yourself. If you come up with something odd, stupid or clearly inappropriate, it doesn't matter. Write it down anyway. Keep going until you have at least 30 items on your list – and do your best to make sure you have your list complete within five minutes. Number the items as you write them down so that you know when you've got your full 30.

Once your list is full, go back through it and select the six best answers – the ones you feel make the most sense and give you the greatest insight. If you have coloured pens or felt-tips around, write the six out on a fresh piece of paper in the Sephira's colour. Put it aside. You'll do a different Sephira each time you run through this exercise, and can keep the resulting pages together if you so wish.

Analysis and discrimination are Hod's greatest strengths, and brainstorming like this on the Tree of Life will strengthen your connection to Hod, and also help bring its energies into balance within you. You can use this technique to brainstorm any topic that you need insight or ideas for, from a new logo to good Christmas presents.

RIGHT: **Brainstorming is the time-proven key to unlocking your creative power and energy – and it's surprisingly good fun too.**

The Transcendental Om

SPHERE: *Hod*

BENEFITS: *Increase personal awareness, generate healing energy*

FREQUENCY: *Daily*

DURATION: *Four weeks*

MAINTENANCE: *Once-weekly*

This exercise requires a candle, which should be lit and placed four or five feet (1.5 metres) away from where you are sitting. Make sure you are comfortable, and won't be disturbed for five minutes. Close your eyes and take several slow, deep breaths, then open your eyes again and gaze at the candle flame. Keep looking at it, but don't stare; allow yourself to blink naturally.

Take a deep breath, and as you do so, imagine white

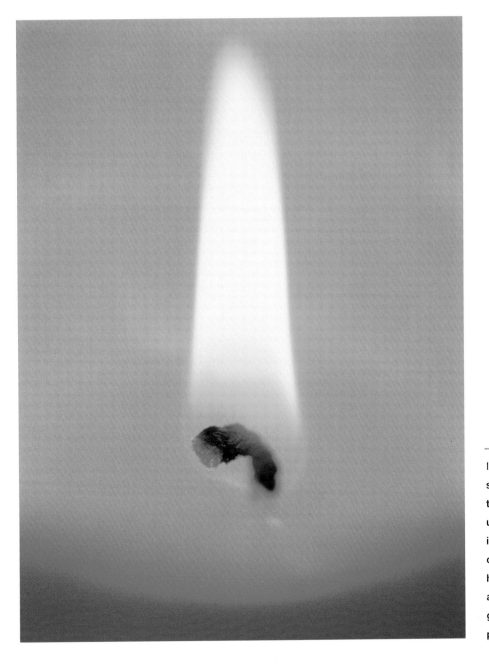

LEFT: **By making a strong connection to the energy of the universe, you will improve your outlook, your health and your life, and spread goodwill to the planet.**

energy from all around you – particularly the candle – flowing in through your mouth and down into your heart. It makes your heart glow brightly. Very slowly, resonate the syllable "Om." The sound of it changes as you speak it – it sounds like "Ah-oo-mm-nnn," or AUMN. As you start exhaling, you begin with the "ah" sound of the A, and the glow in your heart intensifies. The glow rises as you exhale, and as it reaches your throat, you are vocalizing the "oo" sound of the U. The glow continues to rise, and as it reaches the back of your throat, and the sound hits your lips, it becomes the "mmmm" sound of the M. Finally, as the energy continues to rise toward your third eye, the sound changes to the resonant "nnnnn" of the N. Hold that until all your breath is exhaled.

You should then do something with the positive energy you have gathered – either send it out into the world in general as a healing force, or beam it at someone in specific who you know needs healing, in your presence or not.

You can also use the energy to help smooth your way to fulfilling a desire by imagining a simple symbol to represent that desire and then pouring the energy from your forehead into that symbol.

A Walk in the Park

SPHERE: *Netzach*
BENEFITS: *Brings peace and calmness, very empowering, links strongly to Netzach*
FREQUENCY: *Once or twice a week*
DURATION: *A month*
MAINTENANCE: *Cut-down version daily*

Before you start this exercise for the first time, take a moment or two to relax and locate the place within your own body where you feel that your true self resides.

Sit still, breathe slowly and deeply, close your eyes, and hunt for the core of your sense of "I". Because we are such visual creatures, many of us feel that our centre of self is the spot just between the eyes, at the bridge of the nose. However, the sense of self can be anchored at any position in the body, from the crown of the head to the tip of the right toe – even, in some rare individuals,

outside the body itself. When you have identified your centre of self, picture it as clearly as possible, and make a mental note of it.

When it comes to the exercise proper, take the title literally, and find a piece of attractive park or countryside that you can get to. Specifically, you need to be able to walk among trees, and have cars, crowds and buildings out of sight at the very least – preferably out of hearing range, too. If it is genuinely impossible for you to get to a piece of parkland even once a week for a month then you'll have to make do with finding somewhere attractive that is as natural as you can manage.

Once you are in position at the start of your natural setting, think for a moment about your centre of self. Focus all your attention on that point. Recognize that all the textures and qualities of your being come from that point – happiness, sadness, love, stress, truthfulness, and so on. It is where your personality flows from. The spot itself, however, is totally free of all that content. It is calm, silent, centred and pure. Your emotions drive out from the spot, but do not enter within it. This is the locus of your true self, the point from which you emanate, and it is in perfect peace.

Concentrate on that feeling of peace and centred silence, and start walking through the park. Allow yourself to be aware of the nature around you, the beauty and energy of it, but focus your mind entirely on your centre. If you feel your awareness of your centre starting to slip, if you lose the calm of it, then stop walking and re-focus yourself before continuing. Keep walking for 20 minutes, enjoying the beauty outside and the calm within.

During the rest of the week – and after the main period – try as much as possible to get into the habit of centring yourself in your true seat during your everyday life. Any time you start moving around, re-invoke the awareness of calm completion. Bring it into your life as much as possible. It is the true essence of Netzach, and focusing on it will make it much easier to cope with, and take control of, your everyday life.

RIGHT: **By getting away from the bustle of modern life, we are able to find our centre of inner peace and stability.**

Receptive Art

SPHERE: *Netzach*

BENEFITS: *Heightens and balances connection to Netzach, boosts creativity*

FREQUENCY: *Two to three times weekly*

DURATION: *Three weeks*

MAINTENANCE: *Once every two weeks*

This exercise is simple, but does require a certain amount of preparation in terms of materials. Before starting you need to pick a type of art or artistic craft that seems like fun to you, and get hold of the materials required for it. You don't have to be any good whatsoever at the art in question, just so long as the idea appeals to you. The only restriction is to avoid working with words, because that engages different areas of the brain. Common choices for people without any particular artistic ability include sculpting with modelling putty, creating collages, colouring and so on. It doesn't matter if you last did the activity you select when you were 12; in fact, quite the opposite. This is a great chance to just play for a while and have fun.

When you have half an hour free, assemble your art materials, still your mind, and concentrate your thoughts on Netzach. Don't plan anything, just play around with your materials. Let your body go ahead and tinker with stuff while your conscious mind concentrates on stilling itself. It couldn't matter less if all you manage to make is an unholy mess. Let Netzach's influence guide you artistically without worrying about irrelevancies like quality or theme. Just let yourself go, and relax into the exercise.

After you've finished, put the result aside and tidy up. You don't have to show it to anyone if you don't want to, but you should make a point of keeping it. Have a look at it any time you need to remind yourself that yes, you are allowed to be silly and just have fun sometimes.

LEFT: **Forget 'experts'. Art is not about mastery or perfection, it is about the joy of the act of creation itself.**

RIGHT: **Self-determination is the key to gaining control and leverage over your own life. Take charge.**

The Sorcerer

SPHERE: *Tiphareth*

BENEFITS: *Strong link to Tiphareth, highly empowering*

FREQUENCY: *Several times daily (takes about 20 seconds)*

DURATION: *Four weeks*

MAINTENANCE: *Ideally, keep on as before*

The Sorcerer is an extremely quick and easy exercise that can, and should, be performed anywhere, any time you can close you eyes for 20 seconds. To perform it, close your eyes, take a slow, deep breath, and say to yourself: "I am a Sorcerer. Everything I see, I create. I have created, am creating and will continue to create my own world." Open your eyes again and look around. Think about the implications for a moment – that your own choices and actions have brought you to where you are right now, that they keep you where you are, and that your future depends entirely upon you and your choices to come. Accept the simple, literal truth of the statement.

Repeat this as often as possible, particularly in situations that you are dissatisfied with, or where you are feeling powerless.

The Guardian Angel

SPHERE: *Tiphereth*

BENEFITS: *Improves rapport with immortal Self, balances Tiphereth energies, access to wellspring of creativity and good advice*

FREQUENCY: *Two to three times a week*

DURATION: *Four weeks*

MAINTENANCE: *Full session once or twice every two weeks*

Make sure you have 20 minutes in which you will not be disturbed. Sit or lie down, make yourself comfortable, close your eyes and take several long, slow, deep breaths. When you are relaxed, clear your mind of thoughts and concentrate on your centre of being from the Walk in the Park exercise. Clearly visualize the following:

You are standing comfortably in your personal centre, calm and perfectly centred. In front of you, visualize a mirrored elevator door. Reach out and press the up button. There is a moment's pause, and then a harmonious, multi-tonal ping noise, and the doors open. Walk into the elevator, and notice that there are three buttons. The top one is marked S, the middle one is marked C, and the lowest one is marked U. The computerized indicator above the doors reads "C". You reach out and press the "S" button. The doors slide closed smoothly, and the lift starts moving slowly upward. Floor numbers tick past on the indicator as you watch – 1 … 2 … 3 … 4 … 5 … 6 … 7 … 8 … 9 … 10. The lift stops smoothly, pings harmoniously again, and the doors open. As they do, brilliant white light floods in, brighter than anything you've ever seen. Somehow, it does not pain or blind you. Facing into the light, you wait until the doors open, and step out to join the being you've come to meet…

What happens next varies from individual to individual. The light dims a bit, and you can see you are in a room with a friendly person. I can't even begin to guess what sort of room you will see, however, or what form the person will take. The being is the representation of your highest Self, your immortal soul, and you are its reflection in the world at this time. Keeping your mind totally still, enter into a conversation with the being. Feel free to ask it anything you want; for some topics it will be able to offer you advice, wisdom or knowledge. It is particularly useful in guiding you toward your correct path. If it tells you its name, keep it utterly secret forever.

To be certain you've arrived at the right place each

ABOVE & RIGHT: **Using the familiar imagery of a lift will allow you to access areas – levels – of your mind that you could not normally reach.**

time, remember to run a few double-checks. Any advice or comment should be ultimately positive rather than negative. Your guardian angel may be severe with you at times, even tell you things that are uncomplimentary, but it will never be done negatively or with judgement. Anything you are told should help you expand and extend, not diminish you. It is a loving parent, not a jealous teacher or angry priest. Trust your feelings on the accuracy of the scene. Does it seem right? Does anything feel off? If you are in the right place, you will have no doubt about it.

When you've finished, walk back into the lift (the doors are still open), and press the C button. The floors will count back down from 10 to 1, and then you can step out into your perfect centre. Feel yourself expanding back into your whole body, and open your eyes.

Remember to keep detailed notes of each visit you pay to your guardian angel. Some details may change from time to time – they might be a hint of some sort. All sorts of comments or images may only become clear as time passes, perhaps even after the event that they refer to.

with the first row but pointing the other way. Keep going, concentrating fully on what you are doing, until you have counted all the matches out of the box, and made a perfectly regular stack with them.

As soon as you have finished, remove the last match from the stack and place it back into the matchbox, counting back down again. Continue counting the matches back into the box again, slowly and deliberately, one by one. Maintain high concentration as you do so. When all the matches are back in the box, set the box aside for reuse over the following four weeks.

By training your will and patience with pointless tasks, you gain authority and confidence to do what is right under pressure. That brings you in line with Geburah, and also means that when you actually need willpower – to make an unpleasant choice, for example, or to assert your own needs – you will have that much more strength with which to do it.

BELOW: **Repeating a tedious action purely for the sake of it is a good way of strengthening the will.**

Will Training

SPHERE: *Geburah*
BENEFITS: *Strong link to Geburah, great boost to personal willpower*
FREQUENCY: *Once a day*
DURATION: *Four weeks*
MAINTENANCE: *Once a week*

For this exercise, you'll need a box of matches and a few minutes during which you can guarantee that only a genuine matter of life and death will interrupt you. Open the box of matches, take a slow breath, and still your mind.

Remove the matches from the box one at a time, slowly and deliberately. Count them as you go. Place them in tightly-packed rows of five, with the ends lined up perfectly straight, the same way up. Put the sixth match across the first five, turning it 90 degrees from the first ones. Make another row of five, then start the third row turned through 90 degrees again, so that it is aligned

Re-Imagining

SPHERE: *Geburah*
BENEFITS: *Boost self-esteem and assertiveness, increase understanding of Geburah*
FREQUENCY: *Once a day*
DURATION: *Four weeks*
MAINTENANCE: *Once a week*

This exercise requires no preparation. Sit or lie down somewhere comfortable, close your eyes, and take several slow, deep breaths. Think back to a time in your past where lack of resolve, assertiveness, willpower or courage meant that you missed out on something, messed something up, accepted some chore you didn't want to do or otherwise created a problem or made a mistake. Once you've identified a suitable memory, think back over the situation from start to finish in as much

BELOW: **The past is just a ghost of memory. Rewrite your history and you rewrite your reality. Memory is known to be mostly wrong about the details anyway.**

detail as you can.

Now, once the memory is complete, go over it again with full concentration and visualization. This time, edit the memory as you go. See yourself full of confidence and power. When you get to the point where your will failed you last time, see yourself make the empowered choice. Run through the rest of the scene, making it up as you go along. In your image, everything turns out ideally for everyone concerned. No one is left hurt or disappointed, and you get the best possible outcome for yourself. Really concentrate on this, visualize as clearly as possible, and still your internal dialogue, so that there's no little weasely voice in the back of your head going "…but." As you go through the revised version, tell yourself that this is the true memory, this is what really happened. If there were possible long-lasting consequences, play them out to your best advantage in your memory editor too.

This technique really does work to edit out bad memories and sources of poor confidence and self-esteem. Scientists have calculated that as much as 82 per cent of our memory is false – so who is to say what is real anyway? You can re-image any part of your life for any quality you feel you lacked, not just lack of willpower, but obviously edits that do not involve willpower are less directly centred in Geburah. If you positively re-image one negative memory a day for four weeks, I guarantee that you'll feel – and be – significantly more confident, positive and assertive by the end of the period.

Random Kindness

SPHERE: *Chesed*
BENEFITS: *Strong link to Chesed, boost to self-esteem*
FREQUENCY: *At least once a day*
DURATION: *Four weeks*
MAINTENANCE: *Try to make it a general life habit*

All you need for this exercise is a source of strangers – something that should be in plentiful supply for the vast majority of readers. At least once a day – more if the

opportunity presents itself – make a point of going up to a total stranger and complimenting them in a pleasant, non-threatening way. Congratulate them on a particularly eye-catching item of clothing or a good hairstyle, for example – something that you sincerely do like about them. Smile at them as you do so. To minimize the possibility of appearing to flirt with the person concerned, remain casual, and don't wait around expectantly afterward. You may like to make a point of selecting people who look in need of a little self-esteem, or who are so wrapped up in themselves that they rarely realize there's a world out there at all. Even just saying "Hey, great coat," to someone as you walk past them will do.

By passing on positive energy and making someone feel good about themselves, you are making a very strong connection to Chesed. Paradoxically, it also increases your own sense of self-worth – we are wired to feel good about ourselves when we give selflessly, and being smiled at is always a very positive, self-reinforcing experience. Try to give as much positive energy out as you can – energy you pass out tends to return threefold.

Responsive Meditation

SPHERE: *Chesed*
BENEFITS: *Source of inspiration, promotes intuitive abilities*
FREQUENCY: *Two to three times a week*
DURATION: *Three weeks*
MAINTENANCE: *Once every two weeks*

Make sure you won't be disturbed for 20 minutes or so. Get yourself physically comfortable, sitting or lying down. Close your eyes and take several slow, deep breaths. Silence your mind, and clear your mind's eye of all imagery too. Allow the awareness that you are

ABOVE: **If you clear your mind of expectation and only look for what you need to know, your mind can guide you to places you would never have thought of yourself.**

LEFT: **We feel better about ourselves for giving. It makes us richer. Being kind to a stranger is an amazing boost to self-worth.**

prepared to receive guidance to enter your mind. Concentrate yourself on that fact entirely. Centre your mind on that one thought/phrase, and keep your internal chatter quiet.

For the next 15 to 20 minutes, stay still and focus on the thought of receiving guidance while looking out for any imagery or thoughts that may arise in the mind's eye. Pay particular attention, because any impressions you get may be weak or somewhat muddled. Allow them to bide, but do not let your mind start trying to analyze or interpret anything, and make sure you don't let it start talking again. If you get a particularly interesting image, you may want to follow it, and see what unfolds.

All sorts of important information and imagery can be received by silencing the mind enough to be able to hear it, and then being prepared to listen to it. You can also seek inspiration on particular concepts, events or issues by holding the concept in question in mind while keeping the rest of yourself quiet and focused. With practice, you will find that you become more and more likely to come up with interesting insights.

Group Consciousness

SPHERE: *Binah*

BENEFITS: *Good link to Binah, helps develop empathy*

FREQUENCY: *Two to three times a week*

DURATION: *Three weeks*

MAINTENANCE: *Once every two weeks*

Get comfortable, close your eyes and take several long, slow breaths to relax. Visualize a leafy tree, and then zoom your focus in on one single leaf. Project your consciousness into that leaf, and try to merge with it. Concentrate on evoking the experience of being a leaf, of contracting and expanding to breathe, of being blown around in windy conditions, and so on. Try to picture yourself *as* the leaf. When you have some sort of identi-

fication with the image of being a single leaf, let yourself become aware of all the other leaves on the tree. Make an effort to feel them around you, having similar experiences to your own.

When you have developed a sense of all the leaves around you, try to expand your personal consciousness from the leaf to the tree itself. Feel your original leaf still, but also be aware that you are all the others, plus trunk and branch and twig. This is a difficult mental state to achieve, but try to include the sense of self of all of the leaves on the entire tree.

If you manage to get a decent sense of unity across the entire group of leaves, then slowly bring yourself back to your normal awareness of yourself. As you come back to yourself, however, carry that feeling of unity with you. Apply it to the other people around you in your area physically. Feel yourself, but also be aware, if you can, of the selfness of the others, of its proximity. When, and if, you pick up a sense of that unity, try to carry it back into your normal consciousness with you.

This meditation is difficult to attempt, and difficult to explain lucidly. You will find that your understanding of it increases as you practise. It is an important foundation for advanced processes and techniques.

RIGHT & OPPOSITE: **The leaf is individual, but also part of the whole. However, it is no less important in itself for its group component.**

Pushing the Envelope

SPHERE: *Binah*

BENEFITS: *Eliminates minor fears, taps into Binah*

FREQUENCY: *Daily*

DURATION: *Four weeks*

MAINTENANCE: *Once a week*

The precise details of this exercise will obviously vary from person to person. As a first stage, conduct your own brainstorm and compose a list of 30 everyday things that you find difficult to deal with or frightening – things like spiders, heights or saying "no," rather than large outside forces like crime, death and terrorism. When you have your made this initial list, go through and strike out all the ones that you are not able safely to put yourself in a position to face – which will probably be most of them.

ABOVE: **Will-training exercises really help when the time comes to bring yourself to push the boundaries of your comfort and grow stronger thereby.**

Take your revised list, pick the first item on it, and then, during the day, find a way to put yourself face to face with your fear. It will take a certain amount of will to force yourself to do something that frightens you, but if you have been practising. then your willpower you should have no difficulties.

Every day, try and face a different fear from the list, and when you run out, start again from the beginning. You'll feel a real, tangible sense of achievement for proving to yourself that you *can* face the things that scare you, and your confidence will grow as a result.

Also, in the moment of surrendering to the fear and overcoming it by working through it rather than resisting it, you are opening a direct channel to Binah's deepest challenges.

The Mirror Meditation

SPHERE: *Chokmah*

BENEFITS: *Embodies Chokmah, huge self-esteem boost*

FREQUENCY: *Several times daily*

DURATION: *Four weeks*

MAINTENANCE: *Once a day*

This is one of the most beneficial and advantageous exercises in this entire book. As well as connecting you to Chokmah and balancing its energies within you, it will also greatly improve and enhance your self-esteem and sense of inner peace. It is simple and easy, and as such is one of the exercises that your mind will fight hardest to prevent you from doing.

Stand in front of a mirror and look into it. As you do so, imagine that the person you are looking at is filled with all the positive and dynamic qualities that you wish for in yourself. Concentrate on this impression for a moment, and then when you are strongly aware of the good qualities of the face in the mirror, realize that the image in the mirror is nothing more than a reflection of you yourself. So far, so easy. The hard part comes next.

Still looking at yourself in the mirror tell yourself, out loud, "I love you."

We are conditioned strongly in our society that it is not acceptable to feel self-worth. We are taught to place worth in objects and people that advertisers want us to desire, and we feel that we ourselves are worthless

BELOW: **A simple exercise? Ask yourself this – if you cannot love yourself, how can any other person really love you?**

without them. The consumer society demands this viewpoint. It is pathological, however. If you cannot love yourself, then no one can love you. Ignore any anger, resentment or guilt you may have toward yourself for past issues – those things are excuses. Ignore any perversion or foolishness you may feel; that is merely your subconscious trying to stop you. Look yourself in the eyes and tell yourself, out loud, "I love you." If you are compelled to audibly or mentally add a sarcastic comment or put-down afterward, do it again. Aim to do this three or four times a day. It may be horrendously hard to actually manage the first few times, but it is truly worth it. It is the simple expression of the mystery of Chokmah, and the summary of all its lessons – and also a great boost to the personality.

Accept no excuses in performing this exercise.

Cultivating Stillness

SPHERE: *Kether*
BENEFITS: *Strong link to Kether, balances*
FREQUENCY: *Three to four times a week*
DURATION: *Four weeks*
MAINTENANCE: *Once a week*

No preparations are required for this exercise. Get yourself into a comfortable position where you will not be disturbed for ten minutes or so. Close your eyes, and take several slow, deep breaths. When you are relaxed, turn your attention to your physical body. Spend several moments tuning in to all its little sensations and foibles, any lingering sounds or tastes or smells. Tense your muscles up for an instant, simply to feel them all. Then forcefully discard your physical sensations into a ball in front of you, walling yourself off from them. Tell yourself "I am not my body, but that which inhabits it."

Next pay attention to your thoughts. Listen to the mental processes for a moment, and then discard them into a second ball in front of you. Still your mind. Tell yourself "I am not my mind, but that which inspires it." After that, turn to your emotions. Spend some moments becoming aware of your emotional tones and feelings, any lingering moods or tensions that you might have.

Discard your emotions, throwing them away into a third ball in front of you. Tell yourself "I am not my emotions, but that which feels them."

With the three discarded balls in front of you, repeat the three statements to yourself: "I am not my body, but that which inhabits it. I am not my mind, but that which inspires it. I am not my emotions, but that which feels them."

If you are none of these things, ask yourself who it is who is speaking… and who it is who is listening. Enjoy the stillness of the space you are now in, and consider that you are the spark behind both the piece of you that is speaking and the piece of you that is listening. Spend several minutes considering this before reaching out to touch each of the three spheres again, reabsorbing those elements of yourself.

Final thoughts

Any one of the exercises in this last section can help to revolutionize your life. By practising all of them within the framework of the Tree of Life, you have the potential to truly take meaningful charge over your time here on Earth. But that is just the very beginning. Deeper study of the Kabbalah can bring you into closer contact with God, help you to understand the deepest mysteries of creation, and lead you to real fulfilment. Each of the aspects we've touched on in this book is in itself merely an introduction to a much deeper and richer mystery. There are worlds within worlds waiting to be discovered within the Kabbalah's mysteries. You have taken the first steps into the orchard. Where you explore now is entirely up to you.

RIGHT: **In the end, all is light – the perfect, limitless love of God's invention. It is our heritage, and our deserved birthright.**

Resources

For further information and/or instruction in the Kabbalah, Jewish students are best advised to contact a local rabbi from the Jewish Revival or Hasidic communities and ask about recommended teachers. If you do not have links to those communities yet, your own rabbi should be able to point you in the right direction. There are even a few rabbis who are prepared to teach non-Jewish students, so a course of polite, respectful investigation might yield some results. Alternatively, there are a whole host of resources available on the Internet.

The best orthodox Kabbalah training institute is the Bnei Barach World Center for Kabbalah Studies. They maintain a list of authorized Kabbalah trainers world-wide, including seven in the USA, and one each in Canada, Britain and Australia. Check out: http://www.kabbalah.info/engkab/worldwide-classes.htm

Individual trainers often have a less orthodox viewpoint, and run both local groups and correspondence courses. You might like to investigate:

Ian Broadmore of The Kabbalah School (UK) at http://www.kabbalahschool.com

Will Parfitt (UK) at http://www.willparfitt.com

If you prefer to start your researches on your own, there are some extensive websites to be found:

http://torah.search.com/page.cfm/161 is a vast resource of orthodox Kabbalistic material.

http://www.byzant.com/kabbalah contains all sorts of information from a more Westernized viewpoint.

http://www.digital-brilliance.com/kab maintains a storehouse of magickal and post-Golden Dawn Kabbalistic writings.

Last – but not least – you can always contact the author of this book, Tim Dedopulos, at dedopulos@gmail.com

Remember, if you are looking for guidance and teaching, you should conduct your own extensive research on all would-be teachers and teaching centres.

RIGHT: **Josephus Flavius – priest, soldier and scholar – was born in AD37 in Jerusalem. He chronicled the tumultuous events of the first century AD, including the destruction of the Holy Temple.**

Index

Numbers in italics = illustrations

A
Abraham 13
Abua, Rabbi 12
Abyss of Abada 73–5, 77, 88
acceptance 68–9
Agrippa, Cornelius 24, *24*
Ain Soph Aur/Ain Soph/Ain 75
Akiva, Rabbi 12–13, *12*, 16, 73
"The Alchemists" *90*
alchemy 90–2
analysis 40–1, 42
angels 10–12, 26, 36, 78, 114–15
animism 83
anti-Semitism 15, 23
archangels 11, 26
Aristotle 14
assertiveness 116
Assiyah (Manifest world) 77, 78, 79, 92
Atziluth (Divine world) 77–8, 79, 92
awareness 71, 109–10
Azzai, Rabbi 12

B
Baal Shem (Masters of the Word) 15, 19–20, 74, 80, 103
Baal Shem Tov *20*
balance 49
bear dance *89*
bliss 85–6, 87
Bnei Barach World Center for Kabbalah Studies 124
Book of Jubilees 11
brainstorming 108, 120
Briah 77–8, 79, 92

C
calmness 104–6, 110
Cascading exercise 107–8
celebrity Kabbalists 103
change 52
Chi 44
Christianity 15, 16, 21–4, 80
classical Kabbalism 13–14
consciousness 34, 41–2, 64, 73–4
Corpus Hermeticum 22
correspondence, art of 80–1
creation mythology 8, 15, 18, 28, 73, 78
creativity 108, 113, 114, 117–18
Crowley, Aleister *26*, 26–7, 97, *99*
Cultivating Stillness exercise 122

D
Da'ath 74–5
dangers of mysticism 87–8
darkness 56–8
Dead Sea Scrolls 11
dedication 84
defining Kabbalah 6

Deism 83
de Leon, Moses *17*
devil *95*
diamond *62*
discipline 68
D'vikut (cleaving to God) 16

E
ecstasy 70–1, 74, 83, 85
elements 35
ben Eliezer, Israel (the Besht) 19–21
emeralds *45*
emotion 43–4, 65
empathy 118
empowerment 113, 116
enlightenment 73, 76, 84–90
    paths to 88–90
Enoch 11
Essences (Sons of Light) 11–12
evil 12, 16, 76
expansion 52
Ezekiel 10–11, *11*

F
faith 71
fear 120
Five Senses exercise 104
Flavius, Josephus *124*
Fludd, Robert *9*, *23*
Four Worlds 77–8, 79
fraud 103

G
Gabriel 11, 26
Gematria 15, 16, 21, 22, 78–80
Gnostic Cabbalism 21–4
God 73, 92
    and creation 15, 18, 28, 73, 78
    and evil 12, 16, 76
    Gematria and 78, 79
    human experience of 6, 9, 122
    human knowledge of 8–9, 11, 13–14, 75–6, 80, 82–3, 85
    human separation from 35
    love of 68, 80, 103
    many forms of 26
    purpose of 69
    three veils of 75
    and the Tree of Life 31, 32, 35, 37
    unity with 69, 84
    as unknowable 21
    visions of 10
    voice of 70
    word of 71
    see also Sundering, doctrine of
Golden Dawn 25–7, 96–7
grounding 104
Group Consciousness exercise 118
Guardian Angel exercise 114–15

H
Harpocrates *27*
Hasidic Jews *14*
Hasidic Kabbalism 14–15, 19, 20–1
healing 80, 109–10
Hermetic Qabalism 25–7, 80

Hirsig, Leah *99*
Hod, Great Library of *86–7*
Holy Scriptures 12

I
intent 65–6
intuition 65, 117–18
Isaac of Acre, Rabbi 17
Isaac the Blind 16

J
Jerome, Saint *21*, *82*
Jesus Christ 21, 22
Jewish diaspora 18–19
Jews, Hasidic *14*

K
Kabbalah Denudata 17
Kadmon, Adam *15*, *28*
knowledge
    implicit 64–5
    without understanding 74–5
bar Kochba, Simon 13

L
lavender *39*
León, Moses de 16–17
letters, pregnant 79
Levi, Eliphas (Alphonse-Louis Constant) *25*, 25–6, 94–6
light *7*
lilies *59*
Lubavitcher Hasidim 21
Lull, Ramon *21*, 22
Luria, Isaac 18–19

M
Madonna *101*, 102
magic 24–6, 87, 89
Maimonides, Moses 14, 16
Malkuth *36*, *72*
meadowsweet *34*
meditation 87, 88, 103, 104–22
Merkavah School 10–16, *11*
Metraton 11
Michael (Archangel) 11, 36
Mirror Meditation exercise 121–2
Mispar Hechrachi 79
Mispar Katan 79
Mispar Katan Mispari 79
Mispar Siduri 79
modern world 100
Moses 11, 14
mysticism 8, 82–99

N
Nachmanides 16, 17
Nativoth (paths) *7*, 13–15, 26, 30, 64–71, 78–9, 81, 87, 99, 103
    Aleph (Path 11) 71, 79, 99
    Ayin (Path 26) 66
    Beth (Path 12) 71, 99
    Cheth (Path 18) 69, 74
    Daleth (Path 14) 70–1
    Gimel (Path 13) 71, 74
    Heh (Path 15) 70

Kaph (Path 21) 68, 79
Lamed (Path 22) 68
Mem (Path 23) 68, 79
Nun (Path 24) 67, 79, 99
Peh (Path 27) 65–6, 79
Qoph (Path 29) 65, 79
Resh (Path 30) 64–5
Samekh (Path 25) 67
Shin (Path 31) 64
Tav (Path 32) 64
Teth (Path 19) 69
Tzaddi (Path 28) 65, 79
Vav (Path 16) 70
Yod (Path 20) 68–9, 79
Zayin (Path 17) 69, 74
Nebuchadnezzar 10
"no mind" meditation 105–6
Notariqon 79–80
numerology 11, 13, 79

O
occult 25, 80, 96
opal 40
oral tradition 19–21
origins of Kabbalah 8–12

P
Paracelsus, Aurelius Philippus of
    Hohenheim 91
Paroket 73
pearl 58
personality 37–8, 39, 42, 47–8, 64, 67,
    86–7, 90
Pfefferkorn, Johann 23
Philosopher's Stone 91
Pico della Mirandola, Count Giovanni
    22, 22–3, 24
Postel, Guillaume 18
Prima Materia 92
primitive religions 8
progress 68
Pushing the Envelope exercise 120

Q
Qliphoth 16, 76–7, 90

R
Raguel 11
Random Kindness exercise 116–17
Raphael (Archangel) 11, 36
Receptive Art exercise 113
red cord of Rachel 103
Re-imagining exercise 116
Remiel 11
Responsive Meditation exercise 117–18
restraint 69
Reuchlin, Johannes 23
revelation 70
Rising Through the Spheres exercise 88
Romans 12, 13, 14
rose, yellow 46–7

S
sacrifice 49–50, 68
Safed 12, 18, 18–19
ben Samuel Abulafia, Abraham 16
Sanhedrin (rabbinical court) 12

Saturn 56–7
Scholem, Gershom 8, 17
self, higher 66–70, 114, 121–2
self-esteem 116
Sepher ha-Bahir (Book of Brightness)
    15–18
Sepher ha-Zohar (Book of Splendour)
    16–18
Sepher Hasidim (Book of the Pious)
    14–15
Sepher Yetzirah (Book of Creation) 13,
    13, 15–18, 30, 78
Sephiroth (spheres of influence) 7, 13,
    13–15, 22, 26, 28, 30–63, 81,
    87, 99
    Binah (Understanding) 31–3, 51,
        56–9, 69–71, 73–8, 88, 90, 103,
        118, 120
    Chesed (Mercy) 31–3, 49, 52–70,
        73, 76–7, 103, 116–17
    Chokmah (Wisdom) 31–2, 56–7,
        60–1, 70–1, 73, 75–8, 89,
        103, 121
        and enlightenment 88
    Geburah (Severity) 31, 33, 49–51,
        56, 68–9, 76, 103, 115–16
    Hod (Glory) 31, 33, 37, 40–3, 45,
        47, 56, 64–6, 68–9, 76, 80, 87,
        103, 108–9
    Kether (Crown) 31–2, 44, 47, 56–7,
        62–3, 71, 73–5, 77–8, 88–9, 99,
        103, 122
        living by 103, 108, 122
    Malkuth (the Kingdom) 33–7, 42,
        47–8, 56, 64–5, 69, 74, 76–8,
        88–9, 99, 103–6
    Netzach (Victory) 31, 33, 37, 42–5,
        47, 56, 65, 67–9, 76, 99, 103,
        110, 113
        and the Three Pillars 76
    Tiphareth (Beauty) 31, 33, 37,
        46–8, 66–71, 74, 76, 80, 88–9,
        99, 103, 113–14
    Yesod (Foundation) 31, 33, 37–9,
        42–3, 48, 56, 64–5, 67, 69, 74,
        76–8, 89, 106–7
shaman 66, 83, 83
Sheviret Ha Kelim, doctrine of 18
Sons of Darkness 11
Sorcerer exercise 113
soul 37–8, 46, 47–8, 69
Spanish Renaissance 16–17
Spears, Britney 102, 103
Sphinx 54
spirituality 44
Sundering, doctrine of 28–33, 37, 46,
    48, 52, 58, 92
syncretization 80

T
tables, numerical calculation 78
Talmud, scholars of 10
Tarot 93–9
    Book of Thoth 96, 97–9
    de Marseille 94
    Major Arcana 94, 99
    Minor Arcana 94, 97, 99

Rider-Waite 96–9, 96–7
Tarrocchi triumph card 93
teachers, finding 124
temperance 67
Temurah 79
Theosophists 83
Theurgists 83, 89
Three Pillars 76, 92
Tikkun Olam doctrine 18–19
Torah 14–15, 80–1
topaz 47
tradition 6
"Transcendental Magic" 95
Transcendental Om exercise 109–10
transformation 67
Tree of Life (Otz Chiim) 7, 9, 9,
    15, 15–16, 26, 28–81, 28, 29, 30,
    72, 77, 92, 98
    Abyss 73–5, 77, 88
    art of correspondence 80–1
    Da'ath 74–5
    the Four Worlds 77–8, 79
    living by 103
    the Qliphoth 16, 76–7, 90
    and the spark of divinity 28–30
    structure 31–3, 73
    and Tarot 94–6, 97, 99
    the Three Pillars 76, 92
    the Veils of Existence 75–6
    see also Nativoth; Sephiroth
Tree of the Soul 23
triumph cards 93
tulips 55

U
unconscious 37, 38, 106–8
understanding 64–5
unity 28–30, 69
Uriel 11, 36

V
Veils of Existence 75–6
verbena 43
Visconti of Milan, Duke 93, 94
visualization 106, 114–16, 118
Von Rosenroth 17, 29
Voodoo 80

W
Wailing Wall 14
Walk in the Park exercise 110–11
Will Training exercise 115

Y
Yetzirah 77, 78, 79, 92

Z
Za Zen exercise 105–6
Zerachiel 11
Zohar, the 17
Zoma, Rabbi 12

Picture Credits

The publishers would like to thank the following sources for their kind permission to reproduce the pictures in this book.

Absolute Arts: Shoshannah Brombacher: 20

AKG London: Erich Lessing: 27; /ESA: 36

Alamy Images: Ace Stock Limited: 104; /ImageState: 120

Art Directors & Trip: Itzhak Genut:13

Big Box Of Art/www.hemera.com: 38, 105, 106, 113, 114, 117

CIPL: Des Gershon/www.cipl.co.uk: 12

Corbis: Hugh Beebower: 50; Annie Griffiths Belt: 10; /Mark Bolton: 43, 51; /Jose Manuel Sanchis Calvete: 40, 47; /Steve Chenn: 46–47; /Hal Horwitz:34; /Historical Picture Archive: 96–97; Jacqui Hurst: 39; /Michael Keller: 117; /Claudia Kunin: 33; /Laureen March: 116; /NASA: 6–7; /Richard T. Nowitz: 18–19; /Douglas Peebles: 9; /Steve Prezant: 112; /Bill Ross: 123; /Royalty Free: 107, 108; /Denis Scott: 56–57; /Peter Smithers: 59; /Hans Strand: 111; /Zefa/A. Sneider: 121; /Zefa/Masterfile/Boden/Ledingham: 115; /Zefa/Masterfile/J.A. Kraulis: 109; /William Whitehurst: 62; /Martin B. Withers/Frank Lane Picture Agency: 118

Empics: ABACA: 101

Fortean Picture Library: 9, 15, 17; /James Hyatt: 25

Geo Photos: Eddie Gerald: 74

Getty Images: Altrendo: 53; /Dorling Kindersley:̀35; /National Geographic: 48, 62; /Photographer's Choice: 32, 41, 119; /Stone: 58, 67; /The Image Bank: 45, 55; /Time Life Pictures/Mansell: 71

Photos12.com: Oasis: 94

Picture Desk: The Art Archive: 23; /The Art Archive/Eileen Tweedy: 11

Rex Features: 102

The Bridgeman Art Library: Portrait of William Postel (1510–81), from his 'De Universitate', Leyden, 1643, illustrated in 'History of Magic', published late 19th century (litho), Dutch School, (17th century) /Private Collection, The Stapleton Collection: 18; /St Jerome in Penitence, Meloni, Marco (fl.1504–37)/Galleria e Museo Estense, Modena, Italy: 21; /The Sphinx and The Great Pyramid of Khufu at Giza, Old Kingdom, c.2613–2494 BC (Egyptian, 4th Dynasty, c.2613–2498 BC)/Giza (El Gizeh), Cairo, Egypt, Giraudon: 54; /Native American Shaman, Dutch School, (19th century)/Private Collection: 66; /The Penitence of St Jerome, Pietro, Nicoli di (1394–1430)/Louvre, Paris, France: 82; /A Tungusian Shaman (coloured engraving), Russian School, (18th century)/Bibliotheque des Arts Decoratifs, Paris, France, Archives Charmet: 83; /Monk at prayer at Bodhi Temple/Bodhgaya, Bihar, India, Dinodia: 84–85; /Sala di Lettura, built in 1537–88, Sansovino, Jacopo (1486–1570)/Libreria Marciana, Venice, Italy: 86–87; /Bear Dance, Catlin, George (1794–1872)/Private Collection, New York, USA: 89; /The Alchemists, c.1757 (oil on canvas), Longhi, Pietro (1702–88)/Ca' Rezzonico, Museo del Settecento, Venice, Alinari: 90; /Paracelse (1493–1541) (engraving) French School, (16th century)/Bibliotheque Nationale, Paris, France, Archives Charmet: 91; /Josephus Flavius (AD 38–c.101) also known as Joseph Ben Matthias (engraving), English School, (19th century)/Private Collection, Ken Welsh: 125

Topham Picturepoint/www.topfoto.co.uk: 26, 27, 60, 61, 72, 99; /Charles Walker: 4, 5, 23, 24, 28, 29, 30, 77, 92, 93, 95, 98; /Tomas Spangler/The Image Works: 44

Wellcome Library: 21, 22, 70, 75, 76, 78, 81

World Religions Photo Library: 14, 88

Every effort has been made to acknowledge correctly and contact the source and/or copyright holder of each picture and Carlton Books Limited apologises for any unintentional errors or omissions, which will be corrected in future editions of this book.

3 1170 00910 0102